Faculty Retirement in the Arts and Sciences

Faculty Retirement
in the Arts and Sciences

Albert Rees and Sharon P. Smith

PRINCETON UNIVERSITY PRESS

PRINCETON, NEW JERSEY

Library of Congress Cataloging-in-Publication Data
Rees, Albert, 1921–
Faculty retirement in the arts and sciences / Albert Rees
and Sharon P. Smith.
p.   cm.
Includes bibliographical references.
ISBN 0-691-04287-X
1. College teachers—United States—Retirement.
2. Universities and colleges—United States—Faculty—
Retirement.   3. Science and the arts—Study and teaching
(Higher)—United States.   4. Educational surveys—
United States.   I. Smith, Sharon P.   II. Title.
LB2334.R38   1991
331.25′2—dc20   91-10463   CIP

This book has been composed in Adobe Palatino

Printed in the United States of America by
Princeton University Press, Princeton, New Jersey

1   2   3   4   5   6   7   8   9   10

Contents

List of Figures and Tables

FIGURES

TABLES

Acknowledgments

THE WORK by the Project on Faculty Retirement at Princeton University reported in this book began in the spring of 1988 at the suggestion of William G. Bowen, president of the Andrew W. Mellon Foundation, and David Z. Robinson, then the executive vice president of the Carnegie Corporation of New York. At that time, one of us (Rees) was at the Alfred P. Sloan Foundation, and the other (Smith) was at the American Telephone and Telegraph Company. We had worked together on another research project more than a decade earlier. With initial funding from Mellon, Sharon Smith took leave from AT&T and was appointed visiting senior research economist at Princeton, where Albert Rees joined her a year later, on his retirement from the Sloan Foundation.

Our research would not have been possible without the help of many people and organizations. Our first debt is to the three foundations that provided the financial support for the project: Mellon, Carnegie, and the William and Flora Hewlett Foundation. We are also deeply indebted to our four sponsoring organizations: the American Association of University Professors, the Association of American Universities, the Consortium on Financing Higher Education, and the National Association of State Universities and Land-Grant Colleges. They appointed the members of our committee (listed in Appendix A) and helped us secure the cooperation of their member institutions. Perhaps our greatest debt is to the administrative officers at the more than forty colleges and universities that provided data for the project, data that often could be obtained only with much difficulty.

Five student research assistants have made a major contribution to the project, especially to the work reported in Chapters Four and Five. They are Elizabeth J. Carlson, Alan Bradley Howe, Daniel P. Kinney, Alec Levenson, and Susannah Bex Wilson. The work of all but Levenson served as the basis of their senior theses at Princeton.

We have also been helped throughout the project in many ways by the staff of the Industrial Relations Section at Princeton: Kevin Barry, Sharon Becker, Cynthia Gessele, Joyce Howell, Barbara Radvany, and Irene Rowe. All of the programming for the mainframe computer was ably done by Jerene Good. The attractive charts were drawn by Diane Villareal.

ACKNOWLEDGMENTS

While the work was in progress, preliminary results were presented to seminars at Cornell University, Michigan State University, the National Bureau of Economic Research, North Carolina State University, Princeton University, and the University of Tennessee at Knoxville. We are grateful to the members of these seminars for helpful comments.

Finally, we acknowledge with gratitude comments on the draft manuscript and on working papers from William G. Bowen, Ronald Ehrenberg, W. Lee Hansen, Katharine H. Hanson, Peggy Heim, Charlotte Kuh, Sarah S. Montgomery, Robert M. O'Neil, Jack Repcheck, David Z. Robinson, Sherwin Rosen, V. Kerry Smith, and Mary Jean Whitelaw. These careful readers caught many of our errors, though we dare not hope that they have caught them all.

Faculty Retirement in the Arts and Sciences

CHAPTER ONE

Background and Plan of Study

THIS STUDY was undertaken because of the 1986 amendments to the Age Discrimination in Employment Act (ADEA), which will abolish mandatory retirement for tenured faculty members in colleges and universities effective January 1, 1994. These amendments also required that a study of the consequences of the elimination of mandatory retirement on higher education be conducted by the National Academy of Sciences. At the time our study got under way, the Congress had not yet funded the National Academy of Sciences study, and it seemed doubtful that it would do so. The Academy study has since been funded and is now under way. However, because of its late start, its research will not involve the kind of quantitative data collection emphasized in this project. The scope of the Academy study will be broader than ours, covering additional types of institutions and faculties other than arts and sciences. The staffs of the two projects have been cooperating to reduce the overlap between their efforts.

The present study has been funded by generous grants from the Andrew W. Mellon Foundation, the Carnegie Corporation of New York, and the William and Flora Hewlett Foundation. It has been guided by an advisory committee chosen by the American Association of University Professors, the Association of American Universities, the Consortium on Financing Higher Education, and the National Association of State Universities and Land Grant Colleges. A list of the members of the advisory committee is given in Appendix A.

The original Age Discrimination in Employment Act of 1967 protected workers between the ages of 40 and 65. Since almost all institutions of higher education had mandatory retirement ages of 65 or above, it had little impact on retirement rules in higher education. In 1978, the law was amended to raise the upper limit of the protected class to age 70. As a result of concerns expressed by representatives of higher education, particularly concern over the shortage of jobs for young scholars, the effective date of this change as it applied to tenured faculty was delayed until July 1, 1982. Many institutions raised the age of mandatory retirement to 70 before this date; others did so when required by the new law.

The 1986 amendments that will abolish mandatory retirement in 1994 have caused great concern among senior administrators of colleges and universities and others involved with higher education. Henry Rosovsky, dean of arts and sciences at Harvard University, has written:

> No institution interested in preserving quality can tolerate a growing gerontocracy that necessarily brings with it declining productivity. The disastrous effect on young scholars surely needs no elaboration. If ever mandatory university retirement is deemed to be age discrimination, an alternative mechanism will have to be found to accomplish the same purpose. The introduction of term contracts and periodic tests of competence and performance seems logical. None of this is horrible in theory, but the practice would either be hellish or inefficient. . . . Older professors could increasingly keep out the young, and that is bad. Lesser opportunities could lead the young to be ever less interested in academic careers—a sad picture. (Rosovsky 1990, 211–12)

The concerns of administrators can be grouped into four main categories. The first, as in 1978, is the concern that delayed retirements will result in a shortage of job opportunities for new entrants to college and university faculties. This concern has been diminished by recent research that projects a shortage of faculty by the mid-1990s.[1] A second, closely related concern is that delayed retirement will harm affirmative action programs by reducing the number of openings for minorities and women. Most senior faculty are white males, so their retirement tends to increase the representation of other groups. A third concern is that delayed retirement will have an adverse impact on the budgets of colleges and universities. This concern arises because a retiring full professor is usually replaced by an assistant professor or an instructor at roughly half the salary of the retiree.[2] The last and most important concern is simply that in the absence of mandatory retirement, some faculty members will continue to teach longer than they are competent to do so—that classes will be conducted by professors who have not kept up with their fields.

The concerns just enumerated have already led to a variety of policy proposals, of which the simplest is simply to urge Congress to make permanent the current exemption for tenured faculty. Another possibility is for more academic institutions to offer incentive early retirement plans. These, however, can be very expensive, and the faculty members they encourage to retire early may not be the ones the institution would prefer to see do so. Complex questions have also been raised about the legality of some of these plans. A much more radical proposal is to replace academic tenure with a system of renewable contracts for shorter terms or to institute a system of formal posttenure review.[3] Still another possibility is to change the defined-contribution pension plans now widely used in higher education, which generally give stronger financial incentives to delay retirement than do the type of defined-benefit pension plans used in private industry.[4]

This study starts from the presumption that any policy recommendations need to be informed by more knowledge about the actual patterns of retirement in higher education and about the relationships between age and faculty performance. Such knowledge will help policymakers in higher education to decide whether the 1986 amendments to ADEA require far-reaching policy responses, such as modifying academic tenure, or whether more modest adjustments will be sufficient.

To keep this study manageable in scope, it has been confined to the arts and sciences; this is also the principal area of interest of our lead funder, the Mellon Foundation. Faculty members in the arts and sciences are less likely than those in most professional fields to have their retirement plans influenced by the possibility of a second career as a practitioner or consultant. Some of the associations of professional schools have done or are doing their own studies of the effect of the end of mandatory retirement on professional schools in their fields, and in one case we have drawn on such a study.

Our study consists of two rather different parts. The first is based on a set of data on the age distribution of the tenured faculty in the arts and sciences and flows into and out of this faculty from a set of thirty-three cooperating institutions. A list of these institutions is given in Appendix B. The results of this part of the study will be presented in Chapters Two and Three. The second part consists of a set of special studies and surveys done at a much smaller number of institutions, together with some analysis based on surveys conducted by other organizations. The special studies of the relationship between age and faculty productivity are discussed in Chapter Four. Survey data based on surveys of retirees and senior faculty are discussed in Chapter Five. These deal with such matters as the satisfaction of former faculty members with retirement and the plans of faculty approaching retirement age.

We should make clear at the outset that our sample of institutions is not and was never intended to be a random sample of institutions of higher education in the United States. This distinguishes this study from some other recent studies. In particular, we have confined our study to research and doctorate-granting universities and selective liberal arts colleges. This decision was based in part on the advice of our advisory committee as to where the most severe potential problems of delayed retirement might be expected to occur, and in part on examination of data from some earlier studies that showed a strong positive relationship between the selectivity of the institution in admissions and the average retirement age of its faculty.[5]

We also decided to take advantage of the fact that several states have already abolished mandatory retirement of tenured faculty by state law; in some cases, these laws have been in effect for a number of years. At the end of 1989, the states with such laws were Florida, Hawaii, Maine, Texas, Utah, and Wisconsin. Two additional states, Connecticut and Virginia, had abolished mandatory retirement in their state university systems without doing so for private institutions. New York abolished mandatory retirement in public higher education in 1990.

These state laws create a kind of natural experiment, whose results we were eager to observe. We have therefore included as many universities and liberal arts colleges as we could find that are already "uncapped"—that is, have no mandatory retirement age. We have also tried to include some "capped" institutions that were similar in size, type, and geographical location to these uncapped institutions. Finally, because we were dependent on the goodwill of the cooperating institutions in furnishing data that were often difficult to provide, we have included many of the institutions represented on our advisory committee.

A total of forty-two institutions agreed to provide data for this study. Eight of these were unable to provide the data that we requested or provided data that were not usable. One institution that provided good data has been omitted from the analysis because it is in a class by itself. This is Johns Hopkins University, which is the only private university in the original sample that does not enforce mandatory retirement at age 70, and is thus de facto uncapped. This leaves us with a final sample of thirty-three institutions. Of these, fourteen are liberal arts colleges and nineteen are universities.[6] The universities, however, provide many more observations on individual faculty members because of their larger size. The fourteen liberal arts colleges had a total of 1,311 tenured faculty members in the arts and sciences in the academic year 1988–1989; the nineteen universities had a total of 6,412. We requested that institutions omit observations for librarians and athletic coaches even if they had faculty status, and almost all institutions were able to do so.

For institutions having more than one campus with programs in the arts and sciences, we have used data only from the "flagship" campus, the one with the largest number of doctoral programs. For example, our data for the University of Wisconsin are for the Madison campus, and not for the other campuses of the university.

Each institution in the sample was asked to provide the age distribution of its tenured faculty in the arts and sciences for a recent year, divided into three broad categories: humanities, social sciences, and natural sciences. A listing of the departments included in each of these categories is given in Appendix C. For each of these categories, the institution was requested to provide ten or more years of flow data on entries to and exits from the tenured faculty by exact age at the time of the flow. Inflow data were divided into hires with tenure and promotions to tenure, and outflow data were divided into resignations, retirements, and deaths. If an institution was unable to provide ten years of flow data, but could provide at least five, it was kept in the sample. If it could provide data on retirement, but not on other flows, it was also kept in the sample. Some institutions were unable to provide any flow data by exact age, and were dropped from the sample for this reason. Each institution in the sample was also asked to provide copies of its retirement plan documents, of its early or phased retirement plan if it had one, and of policies relating to the benefits and privileges of emeritus faculty.

There is a substantial literature on faculty retirement that predates our study (see Selected References). We shall not attempt to summarize it here. Rather, we shall refer to it throughout the study where it is most relevant. Readers interested in a summary of this literature should consult two recent books: Karen C. Holden and W. Lee Hansen, editors, *The End of Mandatory Retirement in Higher Education* (San Francisco: Jossey-Bass, 1989); and The Commission on College Retirement, *Pension and Retirement Policies in Colleges and Universities* (San Francisco: Jossey-Bass, 1990).

NOTES

1. See in particular William G. Bowen and Julie Ann Sosa, *Prospects for Faculty in the Arts and Sciences* (Princeton: Princeton University Press, 1989).

2. As we shall show later, this happens much more often at liberal arts colleges than at universities. Liberal arts colleges make almost all their additions to the tenured faculty by promotion, while universities hire substantial numbers of people in the tenured ranks.

3. See Oscar M. Ruebhausen, "Implications of the 1986 ADEA Amendments for Tenure and Retirement," in Karen C. Holden and W. Lee Hansen, eds., *The End of Mandatory Retirement: Effects on Higher Education* (San Francisco: Jossey-Bass, 1989). See also the different view of Matthew W. Finkin, "Tenure after the ADEA Amendments: A Different View," ibid.

4. A proposal along these lines was made by David Z. Robinson of the Carnegie Corporation of New York to a conference on college and university retirement issues held in Washington, D.C., on September 8 and 9, 1988.

5. According to a study of retirement patterns in public higher education in New Jersey covering the period 1982–1986, the mean age at retirement was 64.4 at the state university, 63.7 at the four-year state colleges, and 62.4 at the community colleges. See M. Anne Hill, "An Examination of Retirement Patterns and the Age Distribution of Faculty in Public Higher Education in New Jersey" (Bureau of Economic Research, Rutgers University, 1988), table 4.

6. In terms of the classification of institutions used by the Carnegie Foundation for the Advancement of Teaching, all of our colleges are Liberal Arts Colleges I, highly selective institutions that award more than half of their degrees in the liberal arts. All but three of our universities are Research Universities I. The exceptions are the University of Maine, which is Doctorate-Granting II, and American and Tufts universities, which are Doctorate-Granting I. Maine is uncapped; the other two are capped. The difference between a research university and a doctorate-granting one is that the latter gives fewer doctorates each year, often in fewer fields, and receives less federal support.

CHAPTER TWO

Analysis of Flow Data

IN THIS chapter, we analyze our data on flows into and out of the tenured faculty of arts and sciences. The chapter is divided into three sections. In the first, we give an overview of the flow data. The second uses flow data on retirements to explore the effects of changes in the mandatory retirement age. The third uses the retirement data to examine the effects on retirement age of differences in types of pension plans.

AN OVERVIEW OF THE FLOW DATA

Our data distinguish two kinds of inflows, hires and promotions, and three kinds of outflows, resignations, retirements, and deaths. In this analysis, a hire means that a faculty member was hired with tenure, and a promotion means that a faculty member received tenure after previously serving in a nontenured position. Such promotions may involve promotions in rank, but need not. A promotion in rank that does not involve receiving tenure, say, from associate to full professor, is not counted. A few institutions in our sample never hired with tenure; faculty members hired at the rank of full professor received an initial term appointment. All of the inflows into the tenured faculty at these institutions are therefore promotions.

We should emphasize that all our flows are flows into and out of individual institutions and not classes of institutions or the higher education system as a whole. When we report a faculty member as hired with tenure, we do not know whether his or her previous position was at another academic institution or with some other kind of employer. We similarly do not know whether those who resigned did so to join some other faculty or to leave academic employment altogether. For retirees, we are unable to tell which, if any, took postretirement positions at other institutions.

A few of the institutions provided data on separations resulting from disability. Because these were not distinguished from other separations by most of our sample, we have combined them with resignations unless they were explicitly reported as retirements.

TABLE 2-1

Flows into and out of Tenured Faculty, Five Most Recent Academic Years

	Inflows			Outflows			
	Hires	Promotes	Total	Resigns	Retires	Deaths	Total
Universities							
Private	251	354	605	182	289	31	502
	41.5%	58.5%	100%	36.2%	57.6%	6.2%	100%
Public							
Capped	100	240	340	93	185	28	306
	29.4%	70.6%	100%	30.4%	60.5%	9.1%	100%
Uncapped	43	210	253	78	116	12	206
	17.0%	83.0%	100%	37.9%	56.3%	5.8%	100%
Liberal arts colleges							
Capped	22	149	171	37	82	10	129
	12.9%	87.1%	100%	28.7%	63.6%	7.7%	100%
Uncapped	3	79	82	16	44	5	65
	3.7%	96.3%	100%	24.6%	67.7%	7.7%	100%

Note: Percentages are of total inflow or outflow.

We count a person as retired when the employing institution does, although we are aware that in some cases retirement is followed by part-time or occasional teaching. This is usually at the discretion of the institution.

Of the thirty-three institutions in the sample, twenty-five provided data for at least five years on all five types of flows; most of the rest provided data on retirements only. Table 2-1 shows the size of the data base for the five most recent academic years for the twenty-five institutions providing full flow data. The first line in each pair is the number of persons; the second is the percentage of total inflows or total outflows.

It should be noted first that for each class of institution, the number of additions to the tenured faculty exceeds the number of people who left it. We cannot tell from our data whether this represents growth of the total faculty of arts and sciences, an increase in the proportion of the total with tenure, or some combination of the two.

The percentages in Table 2-1 show that different types of institutions have very different patterns of inflows and outflows. The private uni-

TABLE 2-2
Mean Age at Promotion, All Years
(standard deviations in parentheses)

	All Fields	Humanities	Social Sciences	Natural Sciences
Private universities	36.9	38.4	37.0	35.3
	(4.9)	(5.0)	(5.3)	(3.9)
Public universities				
Capped	38.8	40.0	38.2	38.2
	(6.2)	(6.5)	(5.8)	(6.1)
Uncapped	38.0	39.9	36.9	36.9
	(6.1)	(6.1)	(5.7)	(6.0)
Liberal arts colleges				
Capped	37.9	38.6	37.3	37.3
	(5.0)	(5.7)	(3.9)	(4.5)
Uncapped	37.3	37.8	37.8	35.8
	(4.3)	(4.8)	(4.4)	(2.4)

versities make 41 percent of their additions to the tenured faculty
through hires with tenure; the liberal arts colleges make less than 15
percent of their additions in this way, with the public universities fall-
ing between these extremes. Differences in the pattern of outflows are
less pronounced, but the liberal arts colleges have a smaller proportion
of resignations and a higher proportion of retirements than do the universities.

There are also conspicuous differences among institutions within a
given class. Among private universities, the proportion of additions
made through hires varied from a low of 21 percent to a high of 70
percent (excluding one institution with a policy of not giving tenure to
new hires). The proportion of outflows resulting from resignations varied from a low of 26 percent to a high of 48 percent.

For each observation in the flow data, we know the age of the person
at the time of the inflow or outflow. Table 2-2 shows the mean age at
promotion (the largest flow) taken over all years by type of institution
and discipline. This table shows no appreciable differences by type of
institution, although promotion comes somewhat later at public institutions than at private ones. Given the size of the standard errors, none
of the individual differences between means in Table 2-2 is statistically
significant. There is, however, a consistent pattern of natural scientists

11

TABLE 2-3

Mean Age at Hire, Resignation, and Death, All Years
(standard deviations in parentheses)

	Hires	Resignations	Deaths
Private universities	42.5	45.9	56.7
	(7.5)	(8.3)	(8.5)
Public universities			
Capped	42.0	44.0	56.7
	(7.3)	(7.0)	(7.4)
Uncapped	40.4	44.3	58.1
	(7.3)	(6.2)	(8.5)
Liberal arts colleges			
Capped	41.5	46.9	54.9
	(5.5)	(7.8)	(9.5)
Uncapped	45.8	44.7	57.8
	(8.4)	(8.4)	(8.2)

being promoted at a younger age than are the other two groups, and it
seems unlikely that this pattern would have occurred by chance. It is to
be expected in part because natural scientists receive their Ph.D.s at
younger ages than do humanists or social scientists, though in recent
years this may be partly offset by the likelihood that a natural scientist
will have a postdoctoral appointment before accepting a teaching
position.

Table 2-3 summarizes the data for the mean age at hire, resignation,
and death by type of institution. Those hired with tenure are hired at a
somewhat higher average age than that of those promoted to tenure,
and with a larger dispersion. In the private universities, with a total of
534 hires with tenure, the maximum age for this type of inflow is 67,
and almost 20 percent of those hired with tenure were 50 or over. These
data call into question the assumption sometimes made in modeling
the cost of ending mandatory retirement that all retiring professors are
replaced with new assistant professors. It may sometimes be necessary,
in preserving the stature of a department, to replace a retiree with
someone at the peak of his or her career. In such cases, it is not unlikely
that the new appointee will enter at a higher salary than that of the
retiree, so that there is no cost saving at all.

The average age for resignations is somewhat higher than for hires,
but not consistently so. The average age at death is in the mid-50s, but
with a large dispersion.

TABLE 2-4
Mean Age at Retirement, All Years
(standard deviations in parentheses)

	All Fields	Humanities	Social Sciences	Natural Sciences
Private universities	66.8	66.7	66.8	66.7
	(3.6)	(3.5)	(3.2)	(4.0)
Public universities				
Capped	65.6	65.7	65.4	65.7
	(4.0)	(4.0)	(3.8)	(4.2)
Uncapped	65.4	64.6	66.1	65.8
	(4.6)	(5.1)	(4.2)	(4.2)
Liberal arts colleges				
Capped	65.3	65.9	64.9	64.2
	(3.9)	(2.9)	(5.0)	(4.4)
Uncapped	64.3	64.3	64.8	63.8
	(2.9)	(2.2)	(3.8)	(3.2)

THE EFFECTS OF CHANGES IN MANDATORY RETIREMENT AGE

Table 2-4, showing mean age at retirement, begins our exploration of the effects of changes in mandatory retirement age. Here there are no consistent patterns by discipline, but there is a very clear pattern by type of institution. The private universities have the highest mean age at retirement by more than a full year. The liberal arts colleges have the lowest, and the public universities fall in between.

Public universities and liberal arts colleges are classified as capped or uncapped by their status at the end of the period. Most of those that uncapped did so some time during the period covered by the data. The dates of uncapping are one in 1976, one in 1978, three in 1980, three in 1984, one in 1986, and two in 1988.

Surprisingly, the mean age at retirement is not higher at the uncapped institutions than at similar capped institutions. Among public universities, the capped and uncapped differ by only 0.2 years, with no consistent pattern across disciplines. In the liberal arts colleges, the uncapped institutions actually have a lower retirement age by a full year. It would be both premature and illogical to attribute this difference to uncapping. An explanation must await our multivariate analysis later in this section.

Tables 2-5 and 2-6 are based on the same data as is Table 2-4, retirements for all years by class of institution. They show the data by single years of age, with the percentage distributions shown in Table 2-5 and the cumulative percentage distribution in Table 2-6. Table 2-5 reveals several peaks in the distribution of retirements. The first of these occurs at age 62, the first age at which a retiree can collect social security benefits on an actuarially reduced basis. This peak is much higher for the uncapped liberal arts colleges than for the other types of institutions. A second and higher peak occurs at age 65. This is the age at which full social security benefits become available. It is also the normal retirement age specified in many pension plans, and was the mandatory retirement age for many institutions before July 1, 1982, the effective date of the 1978 amendments to the Age Discrimination in Employment Act. The peak at 65 is much more pronounced in the liberal arts colleges than in the universities. The final peak is at age 70, the mandatory retirement age for capped institutions after 1982. The size of this peak differs dramatically by type of institution. In the private universities, it accounts for almost one-third of all retirements. In the uncapped liberal arts colleges, it is nonexistent, accounting for only 1 percent of retirements.

It should be noted that in all types of institutions, there are some retirements after age 70, accounting for between 2 percent and 5 percent of all retirements. The highest percentage is in capped liberal arts colleges (5.3 percent). This demonstrates dramatically that the difference between having a mandatory retirement age and not having one is not that in the first case no one teaches beyond the mandatory age. In some institutions, quite a few people do. Rather it is that in the first case the institution decides who teaches beyond the mandatory age, and in the second the faculty members themselves decide. It is our impression that those who have been asked to stay beyond mandatory retirement age at capped institutions are either the most distinguished members of the faculty or those in unusual specialties where it is particularly difficult to find suitable replacements.

The cumulative distributions in Table 2-6 also show large differences by type of institution. If we look at early retirements, those before age 65,[1] we see that they account for only 18 percent of all retirements in private universities, but more than 30 percent of retirements in liberal arts colleges. Fewer than two-thirds of all retirements in private universities took place by age 69, but 96 percent of retirements in uncapped liberal arts colleges took place by that age.

14

TABLE 2-5
Percentage Distribution of Retirements by Single Years of Age,
All Years

| Age | Universities | | | Liberal Arts Colleges | |
| | Private | Public | | Capped | Uncapped |
		Capped	Uncapped		
46	—	—	—	0.8	—
47	—	—	—	—	—
48	0.2	—	—	—	—
49	—	0.2	0.3	—	—
50	0.2	—	0.3	—	—
51	—	—	0.9	—	—
52	—	0.2	0.3	0.8	—
53	—	0.5	—	0.8	—
54	0.5	0.9	0.6	—	1.1
55	0.6	1.9	2.3	—	1.1
56	0.3	0.7	2.3	—	1.1
57	0.6	1.2	1.4	0.8	—
58	1.1	0.5	1.2	0.8	1.1
59	0.8	1.2	1.4	1.5	—
60	1.1	2.1	2.3	2.3	1.1
61	1.6	4.9	4.0	3.8	5.4
62	5.4	5.3	4.6	6.1	16.1
63	3.1	5.6	6.6	8.3	5.4
64	2.8	4.4	4.3	4.5	6.5
65	15.2	10.2	12.1	22.7	37.6
66	12.1	8.1	9.8	9.1	8.6
67	4.7	19.7	6.1	11.4	6.5
68	10.5	8.6	7.5	7.6	3.2
69	5.6	6.0	6.6	6.1	1.1
70	32.2	15.8	22.8	7.6	1.1
71	0.8	1.6	1.7	3.0	3.2
72	0.2	0.2	—	1.5	—
73	—	—	0.3	0.8	—
74	0.3	—	—	—	—
75	—	—	—	—	—
76	0.3	0.2	—	—	—
77	—	—	0.3	—	—
N	(645)	(431)	(347)	(132)	(93)

TABLE 2-6
Cumulative Percentage Distribution of Retirements by Single Years of Age, All Years

	Universities			Liberal Arts Colleges	
	Private	Public		Capped	Uncapped
Age		Capped	Uncapped		
46	—	—	—	0.8	—
47	—	—	—	0.8	—
48	0.2	—	—	0.8	—
49	0.2	0.2	0.3	0.8	—
50	0.3	0.2	0.6	0.8	—
51	0.3	0.2	1.4	0.8	—
52	0.3	0.5	1.7	1.5	—
53	0.3	0.9	1.7	2.3	—
54	0.8	1.9	2.3	2.3	1.1
55	1.4	3.7	4.6	2.3	2.2
56	1.7	4.4	6.9	2.3	3.2
57	2.3	5.6	8.4	3.0	3.2
58	3.4	6.0	9.5	3.8	4.3
59	4.2	7.2	11.0	5.3	4.3
60	5.3	9.3	13.3	7.6	5.4
61	6.8	14.2	17.3	11.4	10.8
62	12.2	19.5	21.9	17.4	26.9
63	15.3	25.1	28.5	25.8	32.3
64	18.1	29.5	32.9	30.3	38.7
65	33.3	39.7	45.0	53.0	76.3
66	45.4	47.8	54.8	62.1	84.9
67	50.1	67.5	60.8	73.5	91.4
68	60.6	76.1	68.3	81.1	94.6
69	66.2	82.1	74.9	87.1	95.7
70	98.4	97.9	97.7	94.7	96.8
71	99.2	99.5	99.4	97.7	100.0
72	99.4	99.8	99.4	99.2	—
73	99.4	99.8	99.7	100.0	—
74	99.7	99.8	99.7	—	—
75	99.7	99.8	99.7	—	—
76	100.0	100.0	99.7	—	—
77	—	—	100.0	—	—
N	(645)	(431)	(347)	(132)	(93)

Another way to look at mean age at retirement is to see how it changes over time. Because there is a lot of noise in the data for individual years, we use five-year moving averages. Figure 2-1 shows these for universities and Figure 2-2 shows them for colleges. The reader should be warned that although in general the data are five-year moving aver-

FIGURE 2-1

Timing of Retirement of Tenured Faculty at Capped and Uncapped Universities

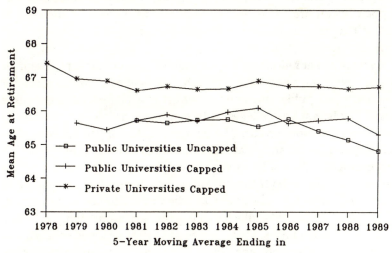

FIGURE 2-2

Timing of Retirement of Tenured Faculty at Capped and Uncapped Liberal Arts Colleges

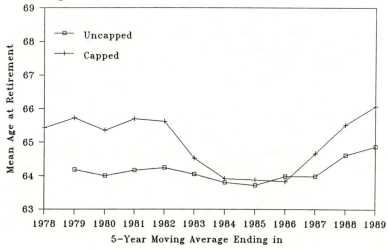

ages, averages for shorter periods may be used when an institution first enters the series. The figures are not based on a constant sample of institutions. In Figure 2-1, there are three capped and four or five un-capped public universities in each observation, except for the period ending in 1989, when there are two of each. The number of private universities varies from a low of four for the period ending in 1989 to a high of eleven for the periods ending in 1984 through 1988. In Figure 2-2, the number of institutions is more stable. There are six or seven uncapped liberal arts colleges in each period, and from three to seven capped liberal arts colleges. The variation in the size of the sample means that the results cannot be unambiguously interpreted as time trends.

Average age at retirement is quite stable through time for the capped public universities and for the private universities. It falls slightly for the uncapped public universities, which is a rather counterintuitive result. For liberal arts colleges, with their smaller data sets, the results are somewhat more erratic. The pattern for the capped colleges is U-shaped, and the mean age at retirement rises at the end of the period for uncapped colleges. However, the uncapped colleges are below the capped colleges at both the beginning and the end of the period. It would, however, be a mistake to ascribe this difference to uncapping. The capped liberal arts colleges as a group are more highly selective than the uncapped ones. Moreover, none of the uncapped colleges had a mandatory retirement age below 70 at any time during the 1980s, while all but one of the capped colleges had a mandatory retirement age of 65 in 1981–1982. In view of this last set of facts, it is remarkable that the mean age at retirement is lower in the uncapped colleges. It will be recalled that the 1978 amendments to the Age Discrimination in Employment Act raised the mandatory retirement age for tenured fac-ulty members to 70, effective July 1, 1982, and that prior to this many of the capped institutions in our sample had lower mandatory retirement ages. (All of the uncapped institutions were either already uncapped or had a mandatory retirement age of 70, and were therefore unaffected by the 1978 amendments.) One therefore would expect to see a rise in the mean age of retirement for the capped institutions at some time after 1982. No such rise is apparent in either Figure 2-1 or Figure 2-2. In plotting median age of retirement, we do see a rise of two years, from 66 to 68, in private universities only, between 1983 and 1985. Over the same years, the mean age at retirement in these institutions rises only 0.3 years. Evidently, the effect on the mean of the higher maximum retirement age was being offset by more early retirements, in part because of the use of incentive early retirement plans.

There are a number of reasons why the effects of the 1978 amendments might not show up in Figures 2-1 and 2-2, even for capped institutions. First, two of the capped universities and two of the capped colleges had a mandatory retirement age of 70 in 1981–1982. For the others, the effect of raising the retirement age takes time to work itself through the system. One can see this most clearly by considering a hypothetical college at which everyone retires at the mandatory age, which was 65 in 1981–1982. The effect of the increase mandated by the 1978 amendments would be that there would be no retirements in academic years 1982–1983 through 1985–1986, since no one would have reached the new mandatory age. Beginning in 1986–1987, one would see retirements at age 70. Under less extreme assumptions, the effect is distributed over the five year period, but even this effect is diluted by charting five-year moving averages.[2]

To try to see the effects of the 1978 amendments more clearly, we have done some additional analysis, using three-year moving averages and classifying institutions by their mandatory retirement ages in 1981–1982. The effects of the amendments still are not revealed. Schools that had a mandatory retirement age of 66 to 68 in 1981–1982 show a strong upward trend in retirement age, but it is as strong before 1981–1982 as after. The larger group of schools whose mandatory retirement age was 65 in 1981–1982 shows no clear trend.

Time series on the flow data for retirements can in principle be used to measure the effect of uncapping on particular institutions by comparing the mean age of retirement before and after uncapping. Unfortunately, only one of our uncapped institutions has a long enough period of flow data on both sides of the uncapping date to make such a comparison possible. This is a large public university with a total of 139 retirements. Prior to uncapping, its mandatory retirement age had been 70. In the three years prior to uncapping, the mean ages at retirement had been 65.5, 66.3, and 65.5. In the four years following uncapping, the mean ages at retirement were 64.4, 66.8, 66.4, and 66.4. Another way of looking at the data is to look at the percentage of retirements occurring at ages 70 and over. In the three years before uncapping, these percentages were 38.5, 16.7, and 23.1. In the four years following uncapping, the percentages were 18.8, 31.3, 21.4, and 13.3. One might conclude from these numbers that in this institution uncapping had little, if any, effect on the age of retirement.

19

TABLE 2-7

Patterns of Retirement of Tenured Faculty—Best-Fitting Regressions

Dependent Variable	Proportion of Retirements at Age 70 or Later				Mean Age at Retirement			
	(1)		(2)		(3)		(4)	
	Coeff.	t-Stat.	Coeff.	t-Stat.	Coeff.	t-Stat.	Coeff.	t-Stat.
Constant	−1.02	−3.42	−1.05	−2.82	56.23	18.91	57.29	15.47
SAT scores[a]	0.098	4.14	0.10	3.36	0.76	3.24	0.68	2.27
Research university	0.21	4.11	0.21	3.16	1.45	2.84	1.64	2.54
Formal early and/or phased retirement plan	−0.054	−0.96	−0.052	−0.89	−0.91	−1.62	−0.96	−1.66
Uncapped five years or more	−0.009	−0.13	−0.010	−0.15	0.014	0.02	0.061	0.09
Defined-benefit pension plan	—	—	0.015	0.15	—	—	−0.49	−0.50
Adjusted R^2	0.56		0.54		0.40		0.38	
N	(31)		(31)		(31)		(31)	

[a] Per hundred points of combined score.

We turn next to the use of multiple regression analysis to explain the variation in retirement ages across institutions. Multiple regression permits us to observe the effect of changes in one variable while holding the effects of other variables constant. Table 2-7 presents our four best-fitting regressions; Table 2-8 gives the means and standard deviations of the variables in Table 2-7, and the ranges of the continuous variables. The number of observations is 31 because data were not available on all the variables for two institutions. The dependent variables in all regressions are based on the five most recent years of flow data on retirements. In regressions 1 and 2, the dependent variable is the proportion of all retirements that take place at age 70 or over. Since this variable draws the line between 69 and 70, rather than between 70 and 71, the purpose of these regressions is clearly not to explain the effects of uncapping. Rather it is to see what forces contribute more generally to late retirement. In regressions 3 and 4, the dependent variable is the familiar mean age at retirement. Regressions 2 and 4 differ from regressions 1 and 3 by the inclusion of an additional independent variable identifying institutions with defined-benefit pension plans. Discussion of these regressions is deferred until the next section.

TABLE 2-8
Variable Means and Ranges

	Mean	Standard Deviation	Maximum	Minimum
Proportion retired at age 70 or later	0.22	0.21	0.73	0.0
Mean age at retirement	65.52	1.78	69.0	63.1
SAT scores	1,198.84	112.99	1,371.0	953.0
Research university	0.52	0.51		
Formal early and/or phased retirement plan	0.68	0.48		
Uncapped five years or more	0.23	0.43		
Defined-benefit pension plan	0.16	0.37		

The first independent variable is the combined mean SAT scores (verbal plus quantitative) of entering freshmen measured for a year at the end of the period and taken from Barron's *Profiles of American Colleges*, sixteenth edition, 1988.[3] In some cases it has been necessary to estimate the mean scores from distributions. Interpreted literally, the score measures the quality of undergraduate students; more generally, it can be considered as a measure of the quality of the institutions on the theory that the best or most prestigious schools generally attract the best students. The variable is highly significant in all regressions, suggesting that professors are more willing to continue teaching when they teach good students or have good colleagues. In particular, we believe that the differences in quality measured by the SAT scores explain the anomalous differences in retirement ages between capped and uncapped liberal arts colleges reported in Table 2-4.

It is also true that the schools with the highest SAT scores tend to have higher salaries than others. We have tried as an alternate measure of the quality of schools the average salary of full professors in academic year 1988–1989 as reported to the American Association of University Professors. The salary variable does not perform as well as SAT scores do. Because the two are highly correlated, when both are entered into the same regression, neither is significant.[4]

The second dependent variable is a dummy variable taking the value of one if the institution is a research university and zero otherwise (three of our nineteen universities are not research universities). This variable is highly significant and has a large coefficient. In research universities, other things equal, 21 percent more retirements take place at age 70 or over, and the mean age at retirement is 1.45 years higher. This suggests that professors are less anxious to retire when a large part of their job consists of research rather than teaching.[5] A dummy variable for type of control (public or private) does not perform as well as one that identifies research universities regardless of control.

Our third independent variable is a dummy variable taking the value of one if the institution has a formal early retirement plan or phased retirement plan and zero otherwise. By an early retirement plan, we mean a plan that offers a special package of cash and benefits to professors who agree to retire before mandatory or customary retirement age.[6] By a phased retirement plan, we mean a scheme that provides part-time pay for part-time service for professors nearing mandatory or customary retirement age, usually with the continuation of full benefits. Just over two-thirds of our institutions have one or the other of these plans or both. Included in the remaining third are those private universities where the dean or provost may make a special early retirement deal with an individual professor, but such deals are not embodied in a formal plan or made generally available.

The variable for early or phased retirement plans is not statistically significant in any regression. Nevertheless, it has the right sign in all, and has a large coefficient (almost a full year in regressions 3 and 4). We suspect that the lack of significance results from the small size of our sample, and that the variable would work—that is, cause a significant decline in mean retirement age—in a large sample of institutions. This is, of course, not at all the same as saying that early retirement plans are worth what they cost. We know of several institutions that have given up such plans because they were too expensive; one medium-sized university has spent more than $2 million on such a plan in recent years. Moreover, we have seen no systematic evidence on whether it is the best or the worst of the eligible professors, or some of each, who take advantage of such plans, and the anecdotal evidence runs in all directions.

Our fourth independent variable is the most important one in terms of the purpose of this study. It is a dummy variable taking the value of one if the institution had no mandatory retirement age during the five-year period covered by the regression, and zero otherwise. Almost one-fourth of the institutions were uncapped throughout the period. For reasons noted above, we should not expect this variable to work in regressions 1 and 2, but we should expect it to work in regressions 3 and 4. It does not. The coefficients are almost precisely zero and are utterly insignificant.

Also included in regressions 2 and 4 is a dummy variable taking the value one if the institution has a defined-benefit pension plan and zero otherwise. This effect is discussed in the next section.

It has been suggested to us by David Breneman of Harvard University that enrollment growth might be a factor influencing age at retirement, on the ground that in institutions where enrollment is growing rapidly, administrators might encourage senior faculty to delay retirement. Malcolm Getz and John J. Siegfried of Vanderbilt University have kindly furnished us with their estimates from HEGIS data of the average annual growth of full-time-equivalent enrollment, including graduate and professional students, from 1978–1979 to 1987–1988 for twenty-nine of the thirty-one institutions in Table 2-7. When we estimate the regressions in Table 2-7 for these twenty-nine institutions, adding enrollment growth as a new independent variable, we find that enrollment growth is not significant and does not have the expected sign.[7]

How should we interpret Table 2-7 as it bears on the central question of the effect of uncapping? We feel that a reasonable interpretation would run as follows: First, tenured faculty members in the arts and sciences retire later when their jobs consist in large part of research, when their teaching loads are lighter, and when they teach good students. More generally, we might say that professors in the very best institutions retire later than those in the next tier down.

Second, we conclude, contrary to our prior expectations, that in selective liberal arts colleges and leading public universities, the abolition of mandatory retirement has no perceptible effect on the mean age at retirement. We are deterred from extending this conclusion to private universities by the fact that there are no uncapped private universities included in the regressions.

THE EFFECTS OF DIFFERENCES IN PENSION PLANS

Two different types of pension plans are in use for tenured faculty in higher education. The first, a defined-contribution plan, is in use in most private institutions and in some public ones. In such a plan a percentage of each faculty member's salary is contributed regularly by the institution to an insurer (usually Teachers Insurance and Annuity

Association–College Retirement Equities Fund [TIAA-CREF]). This contribution may be supplemented by a contribution by the faculty member. The faculty member chooses how the contribution is to be divided among the available investment funds, of which there are now four—TIAA, which invests in long-term bonds and real estate, and three CREF funds: an equity fund, a money market fund, and a bond fund. The institution does not guarantee the faculty member any pension amount. On retirement, he or she receives whatever annuity can be purchased with his or her accumulation.

Defined-benefit plans are used by many public institutions. The institution promises a pension on retirement, the amount of which is determined by a formula based on salary and years of service. The institution funds its pension obligations by making contributions into a state retirement fund, but the amount of these contributions is not contractually specified.

As we noted in Chapter One, it has been contended that defined-contribution pension plans create an incentive to delay retirement. In our sample, defined-benefit plans occur only in public universities. We have therefore classified our public universities by type of pension plan in Table 2-9. Before we examine the table, some further explanation is in order.

A defined-contribution pension plan creates incentives to delay retirement because the amount of the eventual annual pension rises for three reasons: Additional contributions are made during the years retirement is deferred;[8] the prior accumulation continues to earn income during these years; and the life expectancy of the annuitant is shorter at retirement, giving a larger annuity from a given accumulation.[9]

It should be pointed out, however, that the defined-benefit plans used in higher education, unlike those for blue-collar workers in industry, also create incentives to delay retirement.[10] A typical defined-benefit formula in higher education would provide an annual pension equal to, say, 2 percent of highest three years' average salary times years of service. About one-fourth of the states place some upper limit on the amount generated by their formulas; most of these limits are between 75 percent and 90 percent of final average salary.[11] Such a limit is too high to be binding for the great majority of retirees, since it is not reached until at least thirty-seven years of service in the same pension system. Deferring retirement increases both years of service and highest three years' average salary, especially in periods of inflation.[12]

24

TABLE 2-9
Mean Age at Retirement from Public Universities by Type of
Pension Plan

	Mean Age	Standard Deviation	Number of Retirements
Five institutions			
Defined-contribution plan	65.5	4.4	159
Defined-benefit plan	65.8	3.7	437
Eight institutions			
Defined-contribution plan	66.0	4.3	206
Defined-benefit plan	65.3	4.3	572

The highest limit we have seen on pension benefits in a defined-benefit plan is 100 percent of final salary. There is no such limit in a defined-contribution plan. Our survey data (see Chapter Five) suggest that some retirees receive more that 100 percent of final salary, perhaps in part because of the large increase in stock prices in recent years. Such a situation could create an incentive to begin retirement to increase current income; we cannot be sure because we do not know whether in fact faculty members nearing retirement seek to maximize income or wealth.

Our sample includes three public universities that have defined-benefit plans only and two public universities with defined-contribution plans only. There are three public universities in the sample that originally had only defined-benefit plans and subsequently added defined-contribution plans as an option. In Table 2-9, the first two rows, labeled "five institutions," omit the three institutions that offer a choice; the last two rows, labeled "eight institutions," assign the universities offering options to one of the two plans. This can be done on the basis of the length of time the option has been offered. One of these universities has had this option for sixty years and reports that almost all faculty members choose it. This institution has been included among those with defined-contribution plans in row 3. The other two universities added the option in 1977 and in 1984, respectively. Although the defined-contribution option may be popular with new faculty members, the great majority of those retiring in the 1980s would have been covered by the original defined-benefit plan. We therefore include these universities among those with defined-benefit plans in the last row.[13]

25

In the comparison among the institutions that do not offer an option, the mean age at retirement is higher in the institutions with defined-benefit plans, but by only 0.3 years, a difference too small to be of either statistical or practical significance. In the comparison including the institutions offering options, the mean age at retirement is lower in the institutions with defined-benefit plans by 0.7 years, but again the difference is too small to be statistically significant. We conclude from these data that type of pension plan does not have a clear or strong effect on age at retirement.[14]

We now return to Table 2-7 and examine columns 2 and 4, which we neglected in our earlier discussion. These include an additional variable, a dummy variable taking the value of one if the institution has a defined-benefit pension plan, and zero otherwise. As discussed above, the general expectation would be that this variable would have a negative sign. It does in only one of the two regressions, and in neither is it significantly different from zero. It should also be noted that the addition of the variable does not improve the regressions. The adjusted R-squared goes down, and so do the t-values on most of the other variables.

The inclusion of the defined-benefit variable in these regressions is a somewhat different test than that used in Table 2-9. Table 2-9 uses a strict control on the type of institution (public universities only), but no other controls. The dummy variable in Table 2-7 distinguishes public universities with defined-benefit plans from all other institutions, but in the presence of a number of other controls. In neither case does the type of pension plan seem to make a significant difference in retirement behavior. We conclude from the data on retirement flows that the effect of the type of pension plan on age at retirement that has been predicted on the basis of a priori reasoning is not nearly as important as was expected. However, we shall see in Chapter Five that there is evidence from survey data that the type of pension plan does influence the age at which active faculty say they expect to retire.

NOTES

1. No institution in our sample had a mandatory retirement age below 65 at any time during our sample period.

2. We are indebted to Professor Nicholas Kiefer of Cornell University for first pointing this out to us.

3. Barron's receives these scores from the institutions, since the Educational Testing Service, which conducts the test, will not release them. It is possible that some institutions omit some students from their reported averages.

4. It is reasonable to assume that the size of pension contributions as well as the level of salaries would affect the retirement decision. We have run regressions like those in Table 2-7 confined to institutions with defined-contribution pension plans and included as a variable the amount contributed to the plan as a percentage of the salary of a full professor. Although this variable was difficult to construct, it did nothing to improve the regression results.

5. As we shall report in Chapter Four, in 1989 professors in research universities spent more than twice as much time on research as did professors in liberal arts colleges (20.5 hours per week compared to 9.8) and spent less time teaching (20.4 hours compared to 29.3). Faculty in doctorate-granting universities were between these numbers for both activities.

6. See Jay L. Chronister and Thomas R. Kepple, Jr., *Incentive Early Retirement Programs for Faculty* (ASHE-ERIC Higher Education Report no. 1, 1987); and Craig E. Daniels and Janet D. Daniels, "Voluntary Retirement Incentive Options in Higher Education," *Benefits Quarterly* 6, no. 2 (2d quarter, 1990): 68–78.

7. As an alternative to the regression analysis used in producing Table 2-7, it has been suggested that we should use event history, or "hazard" analysis. In such an analysis, the probability of the occurrence of the retirement "event" for an individual tenured faculty member would be specified as a function of certain explanatory variables. These variables would measure influences on the retirement decision from both the individual side (for example, health, income, and attitude toward work) and the institutional side (for example, working conditions and the availability of an early retirement plan). See Paul D. Allison, *Event History Analysis Regression for Longitudinal Event Data* (Beverly Hills: Sage Publications, 1984).

To estimate such a model, we would have to construct a separate observational record for each unit of time in which an individual faculty member is "at risk" of retiring. The appropriate time unit is an academic year, which means that we would have to reconstruct the entire age distribution for each year in which there were retirements.

After some exploration, we have concluded that event history analysis is not a fruitful procedure for our research. First, we have very little data on individuals, and in particular, none on health or on individual salaries or attitudes. Second, although we have current age distributions, our ability to reconstruct previous age distributions, as will be discussed in Chapter Three, is only approximate, and event history analysis requires highly accurate distributions.

8. The federal Omnibus Budget Reconciliation Act of 1986 prohibits employers from reducing or discontinuing contributions to pension plans for employees who continue to work beyond normal retirement age. This provision

became effective January 1, 1988. Prior to that time many universities discontinued contributions when faculty members reached the age of 65 or 68.

9. Some of the incentive to delay retirement provided by defined-contribution pension plans may be offset by changes in the taxation of pension income made in the Tax Reform Act of 1986. These provide that a person who does not take a distribution from a qualified pension plan beginning April 1 of the calendar year following the calendar year in which he or she attains age 70½ is subject to a penalty tax of 50 percent on the minimum amount that should have been distributed. The minimum amount is based on contributions made since December 31, 1986, and earnings accruing on all accumulations since December 31, 1986. This penalty tax does not apply to employees of public institutions.

It is also possible, as David Z. Robinson of the Carnegie Commission on Science, Technology, and Government has pointed out to us, for a person to be drawing an annuity under one contract and at the same time be accumulating under a second contract, perhaps at another institution.

10. Pension plans for blue-collar workers usually provide a fixed dollar, or "flat," amount per year of service. While this amount may be increased from time to time, especially through collective bargaining, there is no formal link to the level of wages. See Zvi Bodie, "Pensions as Retirement Income Insurance," *Journal of Economic Literature* 28 (March 1990): 28–49.

11. See Teachers Insurance and Annuity Association, *Public Retirement Systems* (summaries of public retirement plans covering colleges and universities, 1987), table 4.

12. See W. Lee Hansen and Karen C. Holden, *Mandatory Retirement in Higher Education* (unpublished report for the U.S. Department of Labor, Department of Economics, University of Wisconsin, 1981).

TIAA-CREF has done an illustrative calculation of the gain in the replacement ratio (ratio of pension income to final salary) from delaying retirement for typical defined-benefit and defined-contribution plans chosen so that they have the same replacement ratio at age 65. For a faculty member with thirty years of service under the plan at age 65, the replacement ratio rises from 62.8 percent at age 65 to 83.3 percent at age 70 under the defined-contribution plan and from 62.8 percent to 71.8 percent under the defined-benefit plan. It is assumed that salary rises at 6 percent per year; a higher rate of increase would improve the relative performance of the defined-benefit plan. See *Research Dialogues*, no. 24 (January 1990).

13. The information in this paragraph was obtained from TIAA-CREF (letter from Peggy Heim, senior research officer, dated December 28, 1989), and from conversations with staff of university personnel departments.

14. This is a different conclusion than that reached by Lozier and Dooris, who find mean age at retirement higher by more than two years in institutions with defined-contribution plans. However, Lozier and Dooris do not control for type of institution. Of the fourteen defined-benefit institutions in their

study, only two are doctorate granting. Thus, their results are not inconsistent with a finding of no significant difference among public universities. See G. Gregory Lozier and Michael J. Dooris, *Faculty Retirement Projections beyond 1994: Effects of Policy on Individual Choice* (Boulder, Colo.: Western Interstate Commission for Higher Education, 1991).

CHAPTER THREE

Age Distributions of the Tenured Faculty

IN THIS chapter, we examine our data on the age distributions of tenured faculty in the arts and sciences. Our data all refer to academic year 1988–1989. We distinguish these by type of institution, by discipline, and by capping status.[1] These age distributions become the building blocks for projections obtained by using the Faculty COHORT Model.[2]

The size and timing of the effect of a potential change in retirement behavior that results from the uncapping of tenured faculty is, of course, critically dependent on the magnitude and pattern of the other components of turnover of tenured faculty discussed in Chapter Two. It is also contingent on the current composition of the tenured faculty by age. Although there are data on the age distribution of faculties at various dates from a number of sources, many of these data pertain to all faculty, not tenured faculty only, and there is little differentiation by either Carnegie classification or by discipline, and none by capping status.

CURRENT AGE DISTRIBUTIONS

Drawing from a variety of sources, Bowen and Schuster (1986) have suggested that although the age distribution of faculty remained quite stable from the late 1940s through the 1970s, with faculty "widely spread over the various age brackets" (p. 38), a slow aging process has begun and is likely to continue over the next decade or two. An examination of tenured faculty alone suggests that by the beginning of the 1980s, they, too, were spread over a number of age brackets, though their heaviest concentrations appeared in the 36-to-55 age categories. Projections made at that time by the Carnegie Council on Policy Studies in Higher Education (1980) implied that the average age of tenured faculty would rise from 48 in 1980–1981 to 55 by 2000–2001 (p. 26, cited in Bowen and Schuster 1986, 40).

Bowen and Sosa (1989, 16–20) offer a more timely and detailed perspective, as they report age distributions for all faculty by Carnegie classification and by individual departments within the arts and sciences in 1977 and in 1987. They differentiate three cohorts: under age 40; between 40 and 49; and over age 49. They observe a sharp decline in the proportion of faculty below age 40 and a corresponding increase in the proportion of faculty over age 49 during this time period. At the same time, they see greater variation in age structure across disciplines than among Carnegie classifications.

Lozier and Dooris (1991) also provide a current view of faculty age distributions, although their emphasis is on the older age cohorts. They report age distributions from their random survey of 101 participating four-year institutions for all faculty. They distinguish faculty by control (that is, public or independent) and by level (that is, baccalaureate, comprehensive, or doctoral) of institution and by individual discipline in both the arts and sciences and the professional schools for the academic year 1987–1988. They differentiate a number of cohorts: under age 55; individual ages from 55 through 70; and over age 70. Their data suggest that in the arts and sciences only, 76% of the faculty are under age 55. This figure is rather high, but reflects the fact that the data include both tenured and nontenured faculty. This is evident when these data are compared with data drawn from the 1989 National Survey of Faculty conducted for the Carnegie Foundation for the Advancement of Teaching.[3] It appears that among tenured faculty in the arts and sciences in four-year institutions in this survey, only 64 percent are under age 55.

An examination of age distributions from our data suggests broad agreement with these earlier observations.[4] As in the Carnegie data, only 64 percent are under age 55. Although tenured faculty are spread across a number of age brackets, they display a notable consistency with respect to concentration across type of institution, regardless of capping status (see Tables 3-1 and 3-2). As shown in Table 3-1, the greatest concentration occurs in the 46-to-50 age cohort for all types of institutions with the single exception of uncapped liberal arts colleges, where the largest cluster occurs in the 41-to-45 age cohort.

It should be noted that the existence of a mandatory retirement age does not necessarily preclude the presence of active faculty at age 70 because individual institutional rules often allow individuals to work during the year in which they turn 70 but usually require retirement before their 71st birthdays. Even then, exceptions are sometimes allowed, as is apparent in our observation of one active faculty member in a capped public university in the 71-to-75 age cohort. At the same time, however, even in uncapped institutions, the proportions in this

TABLE 3-1

Age Distribution of Tenured Faculty by Institutional Type and
Capping Status, 1988–1989 (percent)

Age Group	Liberal Arts Colleges		Public Universities		Private Universities, Capped
	Capped	Uncapped	Capped	Uncapped	
21–25	0.0	0.0	0.0	0.0	0.0
26–30	0.0	0.0	0.1	0.0	0.2
31–35	3.0	2.9	2.0	3.5	2.8
36–40	12.9	14.2	8.9	13.2	11.0
41–45	19.7	19.2	16.9	17.6	18.0
46–50	20.1	17.9	19.3	20.9	18.3
51–55	16.6	16.8	16.4	16.8	15.9
56–60	15.1	15.6	18.0	15.9	14.9
61–65	10.1	9.4	12.6	7.8	12.2
66–70	2.5	3.9	5.8	3.6	6.6
71–75	0.0	0.2	0.1	0.6	0.0
76–80	0.0	0.0	0.0	0.1	0.0
Mean age	49.6	49.8	51.6	49.8	51.0

TABLE 3-2

Age Distribution of Tenured Faculty by Institutional Type and
Capping Status, 1988–1989 (number)

Age Group	Liberal Arts Colleges		Public Universities		Private Universities, Capped
	Capped	Uncapped	Capped	Uncapped	
21–25	0	0	0	0	0
26–30	0	0	2	0	7
31–35	21	18	37	54	101
36–40	89	88	162	203	391
41–45	136	119	307	272	641
46–50	139	111	351	323	652
51–55	115	104	298	259	566
56–60	104	97	327	245	531
61–65	70	58	229	120	434
66–70	17	24	106	56	235
71–75	0	1	1	9	0
76–80	0	0	0	2	0
Total	691	620	1,820	1,543	3,558

cohort are very small (0.6 percent at most). Indeed, only 0.13 percent of all the tenured faculty in our data set are in this cohort, and less than 0.1 percent of all the tenured faculty are over age 71. Moreover, there are only two active tenured faculty members over the age of 75 present in the data. It is important to note that sufficient time has elapsed since the effective date of the 1978 amendments to the ADEA (July 1, 1982) for all faculty to have aged enough to take advantage of the change in the mandatory retirement age from 65 to 70. Similarly, ten of the twelve uncapped institutions in our data set have changed their status in this respect long enough for faculty to have aged enough to take advantage of this change.

The opposite end of the age distribution is similarly sparsely populated: Only 3 percent of the tenured faculty are below age 36, and of these, only one individual is less than 30 years of age. Again, this observation is not unexpected, since our data pertain to tenured faculty only and the population in these age cohorts are more likely to be awaiting a tenure decision.

The mean age varies across institutional type and capping status from 49.6 to 51.6. These figures are between the average age for tenured faculty observed by the Carnegie Council for 1980–1981 (age 48) and that projected for 1990–1991 (age 52). This observation is thus consistent either with the aging of the faculty projected by the Carnegie Council or with the special nature of our data set, which includes four-year institutions only. Such institutions have been observed to have somewhat older faculties than those of two-year institutions (Bowen and Schuster 1986, 38).

A separate examination of the age distribution by broad discipline category—humanities, social sciences, and natural sciences—within each of the institutional categories (see Tables 3-3 and 3-4) shows somewhat more dispersion across age cohorts, though the greatest accumulation in most instances is either in the 41-to-45 age cohort or in the 46-to-50 age cohort. Looking at the full arrays of these age distributions, slight differences appear: tenured faculties in both capped public and private universities are similarly concentrated in slightly older cohorts than at the other types of institutions; and tenured faculties in the humanities are clustered in slightly older cohorts than in the other disciplines.

These observations are more striking when the data are broken down into the cohorts employed by Bowen and Sosa, as displayed in Tables 3-5 and 3-6 and Figure 3-1. The proportion of the tenured faculty who are over age 49 is 56.3 percent in capped public universities and 53

TABLE 3-3
Age Distribution of Tenured Faculty by Institutional Type, Capping Status, and Discipline, 1988–1989 (percent)

	21–30	31–35	36–40	41–45	46–50	51–55	56–60	61–65	66–70	71–75	76–80
Liberal arts colleges											
Capped											
Humanities	0.0	2.8	11.7	17.1	20.3	18.0	13.9	12.7	3.5	0.0	0.0
Social sciences	0.0	4.4	12.8	23.6	19.7	10.8	16.3	9.9	2.5	0.0	0.0
Natural sciences	0.0	1.7	15.1	19.8	20.3	20.9	15.7	5.8	0.6	0.0	0.0
Uncapped											
Humanities	0.0	2.6	13.5	17.2	16.1	17.2	19.1	9.7	4.1	0.4	0.0
Social sciences	0.0	3.1	14.0	24.9	17.6	14.0	12.4	8.8	5.2	0.0	0.0
Natural sciences	0.0	3.1	15.6	15.6	21.3	19.4	13.8	9.4	1.9	0.0	0.0
Public universities											
Capped											
Humanities	0.0	1.6	8.9	16.0	17.8	17.1	21.4	11.8	5.2	0.2	0.0
Social sciences	0.0	1.6	9.3	18.7	21.1	15.6	16.1	11.4	6.2	0.0	0.0
Natural sciences	0.3	2.7	8.6	16.1	19.1	16.4	16.7	14.2	6.0	0.0	0.0
Uncapped											
Humanities	0.0	2.9	8.7	19.8	21.4	18.5	17.3	8.1	2.5	0.8	0.0
Social sciences	0.0	5.1	16.6	15.8	18.5	15.4	14.0	9.7	4.5	0.4	0.0
Natural sciences	0.0	2.5	14.3	17.2	22.8	16.4	16.2	5.6	3.9	0.6	0.4
Private universities											
Capped											
Humanities	0.0	2.0	8.5	18.1	19.8	16.5	15.5	12.7	6.8	0.0	0.0
Social sciences	0.2	2.9	11.0	19.0	18.5	15.2	15.1	10.9	7.4	0.0	0.0
Natural sciences	0.4	3.6	13.3	17.0	16.8	16.0	14.2	13.0	5.6	0.0	0.0

TABLE 3-4
Age Distribution of Tenured Faculty by Institutional Type, Capping Status, and Discipline, 1988–1989 (number)

	21–30	31–35	36–40	41–45	46–50	51–55	56–60	61–65	66–70	71–75	76–80
Liberal arts colleges											
Capped											
Humanities	0	9	37	54	64	57	44	40	11	0	0
Social sciences	0	9	26	48	40	22	33	20	5	0	0
Natural sciences	0	3	26	34	35	36	27	10	1	0	0
Uncapped											
Humanities	0	7	36	46	43	46	51	26	11	1	0
Social sciences	0	6	27	48	34	27	24	17	10	0	0
Natural sciences	0	5	25	25	34	31	22	15	3	0	0
Public universities											
Capped											
Humanities	0	9	50	90	100	96	120	66	29	1	0
Social sciences	0	9	51	102	115	85	88	62	34	0	0
Natural sciences	2	19	61	115	136	117	119	101	43	0	0
Uncapped											
Humanities	0	15	45	103	111	96	90	42	13	4	0
Social sciences	0	26	84	80	94	78	71	49	23	2	0
Natural sciences	0	13	74	89	118	85	84	29	20	3	2
Private universities											
Capped											
Humanities	0	23	99	210	230	191	180	147	79	0	0
Social sciences	2	34	129	223	217	179	177	128	87	0	0
Natural sciences	5	44	163	208	205	196	174	159	69	0	0

TABLE 3-5

Three-Cohort Age Distribution of Tenured Faculty by
Institutional Type and Capping Status (percent)

Age Group	Liberal Arts Colleges		Public Universities		Private Universities, Capped
	Capped	Uncapped	Capped	Uncapped	Capped
Under 40	13.3	12.7	9.0	13.4	11.3
40–49	40.1	39.0	34.7	38.0	35.7
Over 49	46.6	48.2	56.3	48.7	53.0

TABLE 3-6

Three-Cohort Age Distribution of Tenured Faculty by
Institutional Type and Capping Status (number)

Age Group	Liberal Arts Colleges		Public Universities		Private Universities, Capped
	Capped	Uncapped	Capped	Uncapped	Capped
Under 40	92	79	163	206	403
40–49	277	242	632	586	1,270
Over 49	322	299	1,025	751	1,885

FIGURE 3-1

Age Distribution of Tenured Faculty by Broad Discipline Category

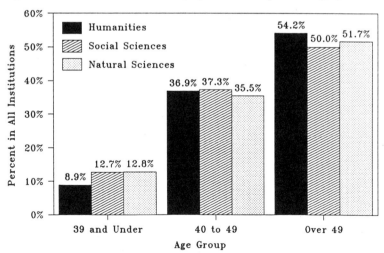

percent in capped private universities, whereas it is less than 50 percent for each of the other institutional categories. When differentiated by discipline across institutional category, faculty in the humanities show the smallest proportion under age 40 (8.9 percent) and the largest proportion over age 49 (54.2 percent). This pattern is consistent with that observed by Bowen and Sosa, though the distinction by broad discipline category is less marked than what they observed at the field of study level.

PROJECTING THE FUTURE

As indicated at the outset of this chapter, the model we use to project the future composition of tenured faculties is Stanford's Faculty CO-HORT Model. This model enables us to project the size and age structure of tenured faculty in the future on the basis of past information on "transition probabilities," that is, the likelihood of individuals (for example, a particular age cohort) moving from one specified state to another over time. The underlying assumption in a Markov chain model such as this is that the faculty behavior (that is, inflows to and outflows from tenure) that results in these probabilities reflects both individual and institutional actions and is characteristic of the subgroups specified (for example, faculty in the 41-to-45 age cohort in liberal arts colleges). In contrast, computer simulation models of faculty planning would make projections over time based on random probabilities that individuals will change in certain characteristics (such as age, institutional association, etc.). Such models have the potential of providing richer projections, but are correspondingly more complex than Markov chain models and require greater detail in data and longer computational time. However, our data do not provide enough information to estimate the probability of changes with respect to each individual faculty member in each institution.[5] Consequently, the Markov chain is more appropriate for use with the data available to us.[6]

The Stanford model calls for the input of data on faculty age distributions in five-year cohorts. In order to be able to highlight the potential impact of changes in behavior beyond the current mandatory retirement age of 70, we define these cohorts as 21 to 25 years old, 26 to 30 years old, etc. This level of aggregation seemed to us to be the minimum that is compatible with our combining of different institutions to form characteristic groups (for example, capped institutions and uncapped institutions). We will make our projections with two different groupings of faculty:

1. faculty differentiated by capping status into two categories—
   a. capped institutions, and
   b. uncapped institutions; and
2. faculty differentiated by institutional type into three categories—
   a. liberal arts colleges,
   b. public universities, and
   c. private universities.

Each of these groupings comprises a subset of the populations discussed above because they include only those institutions that could provide data on all sources of flows into and out of tenure. As shown in Tables 3-7 and 3-8, both of these groupings display a very similar age pattern to those discussed above: Tenured faculty are spread across a number of age brackets, but most show the largest concentration in either the 41-to-55 age cohort or the 46-to-50 age cohort.

Additional inputs to the flow model include tenure ratios, hiring patterns, retention rates, and planned changes in overall faculty size. Because our focus is on tenured faculty, we assume a tenure ratio of 100 percent for each age cohort. Similarly, we include both hires and promotions in the specified "new hire distribution" because either represents an entrance into the tenured faculty. Retention rates are not net of inflows: They are defined as one minus the outflow rate, which is outflows from the age cohort during a five-year period from all sources (resignation, retirement, death) as a percentage of the total population in the age cohort at the beginning of the period.[7]

If all data on all participating institutions were known—including both the current age distribution and the age distribution of five years ago and the actual experience in retention rates, "hires," and changes in faculty size over that period—then derivation of these inputs for projections into the future would be relatively simple and straightforward. However, the institutions did not provide all of this information: They reported the current age distribution and not that of five years ago, and they gave no indication of changes in the size of their tenured faculties.[8]

Instead, we estimate these inputs using the five most recent years of flow data for each of the age cohorts to calculate the changes that are applied to the current age distribution of tenured faculty to yield the distribution of five years ago. For example, to reconstruct tenured faculty five years ago in the 41-to-45 age cohort from current tenured faculty in the 46-to-50 age cohort, we use the data on the inflows and outflows in the most recent five years in the 41-to-45 age cohort.[9]

There are advantages and disadvantages to this technique. The reconstructed age distribution of five years ago is clearly an artificial one. This procedure assumes that the determining factor in flow patterns is the age of the individual involved at the time of the actual flow, regardless of the academic year. It therefore would seem to have more universal applicability and to be more consistent than the alternative techniques (see note 9) with the underlying assumption in a Markov chain model that the transition probabilities are characteristic of the age cohorts specified.

The inflow distributions and retention rates derived from this procedure are displayed in Tables 3-9 and 3-10; base Ns are given in Tables 3-11 and 3-12. The age distribution for inflow and that for retention show many similarities, regardless of capping status (Table 3-9) or institutional type (Table 3-10). For example, inflows tend to be most heavily concentrated in the age 31-to-45 cohorts but also occur in both younger and older cohorts. Retention rates decline sharply after age 65 in all categories but are zero in older cohorts only in capped institutions (and private universities, which comprise a subset of capped institutions).

At the same time, there are noteworthy differences across these categories. For example, although the retention rates estimated for uncapped institutions do show that a portion of tenured faculty members will remain beyond age 70, they also show a far more precipitous drop among the 61-to-65 cohort than in capped institutions.[10] Thus the proportion of faculty who move into the 66-to-70 cohort and who can then decide whether to remain beyond age 70 is far smaller than the proportion of faculty in capped institutions who move into the cohort that ends at the current mandatory age of 70. Similarly, the proportion of faculty who move into the 66-to-70 cohort in private universities is larger than that in either public universities or liberal arts colleges.

These observations suggest that if, with national uncapping, the retention patterns that currently prevail in uncapped institutions were to occur in currently capped institutions, we would see a larger proportion of active tenured faculty over the age of 70 in these institutions than we observe in the currently uncapped institutions. Moreover, we would expect a similar result for private universities.

In order to explore the possible magnitude of these effects, we input the inflow and retention data from Tables 3-9 and 3-10 into the Stanford model. We consider two broad groupings of analyses:

39

TABLE 3-7
Age Distribution of Tenured Faculty—Starting Points for Projections (percent)

	21–30	31–35	36–40	41–45	46–50	51–55	56–60	61–65	66–70	71–75	76–80
By capping status											
Uncapped institutions											
Humanities	0.0	2.5	9.8	19.1	18.5	18.5	18.8	8.7	3.3	0.7	0.0
Social sciences	0.0	3.2	14.6	18.7	19.0	15.3	14.3	10.3	4.2	0.3	0.0
Natural sciences	0.0	2.5	14.5	16.6	21.4	17.7	16.6	6.3	3.6	0.5	0.4
Total	0.0	2.7	12.8	18.2	19.6	17.2	16.7	8.5	3.7	0.5	0.1
Capped institutions											
Humanities	0.0	1.7	8.9	17.1	19.7	16.7	17.6	12.3	5.8	0.1	0.0
Social sciences	0.1	2.4	10.6	19.6	19.9	14.8	15.6	10.7	6.3	0.0	0.0
Natural sciences	0.4	3.4	11.7	16.5	18.0	16.8	15.0	12.8	5.3	0.0	0.0
Total	0.2	2.5	10.4	17.7	19.2	16.2	16.1	12.0	5.8	0.0	0.0
By institutional type											
Liberal arts colleges											
Humanities	0.0	2.4	12.1	17.9	18.1	18.4	16.0	11.0	3.9	0.2	0.0
Social sciences	0.0	4.0	13.3	24.0	19.2	12.3	14.4	9.1	3.7	0.0	0.0
Natural sciences	0.0	2.5	15.5	17.0	20.8	20.8	15.1	6.9	1.3	0.0	0.0
Total	0.0	2.9	13.3	19.5	19.1	17.2	15.3	9.4	3.2	0.1	0.0
Public universities											
Humanities	0.0	1.9	8.4	17.8	18.8	17.8	20.5	10.2	4.1	0.5	0.0
Social sciences	0.0	2.3	11.8	17.6	20.5	15.9	15.6	11.1	5.1	0.2	0.0
Natural sciences	0.2	2.5	10.5	16.6	19.9	16.5	16.9	11.0	5.3	0.3	0.2
Total	0.1	2.3	10.2	17.3	19.7	16.7	17.6	10.8	4.9	0.3	0.1
Private universities											
Humanities	0.0	1.7	8.2	17.5	20.9	15.8	16.3	12.7	6.9	0.0	0.0
Social sciences	0.2	2.4	10.9	19.2	18.9	15.1	15.3	10.8	7.2	0.0	0.0
Natural sciences	0.6	4.2	13.6	16.3	16.7	16.3	13.6	13.0	5.7	0.0	0.0
Total	0.3	2.8	10.9	17.6	18.8	15.8	15.0	12.2	6.6	0.0	0.0

Age Distribution of Tenured Faculty—Starting Points for Projections (number)

	21–30	31–35	36–40	41–45	46–50	51–55	56–60	61–65	66–70	71–75	76–80
By capping status											
Uncapped institutions											
Humanities	0	17	66	129	125	125	127	59	22	5	0
Social sciences	0	19	87	111	113	91	85	61	25	2	0
Natural sciences	0	14	81	93	120	99	93	35	20	3	2
Total	0	50	234	333	358	315	305	155	67	10	2
Capped institutions											
Humanities	2	30	153	294	339	287	303	211	99	1	0
Social sciences	2	39	171	315	320	239	251	173	101	0	0
Natural sciences	7	60	209	295	321	300	268	228	95	0	0
Total	9	129	533	904	980	826	822	612	295	1	0
By institutional type											
Liberal arts colleges											
Humanities	0	13	65	96	97	99	86	59	21	1	0
Social sciences	0	15	50	90	72	46	54	34	14	0	0
Natural sciences	0	8	49	54	66	66	48	22	4	0	0
Total	0	36	164	240	235	211	188	115	39	1	0
Public universities											
Humanities	0	19	83	175	185	175	202	100	40	5	0
Social sciences	0	22	113	169	196	152	149	106	49	2	0
Natural sciences	2	28	118	187	224	186	190	124	60	3	2
Total	2	69	314	531	605	513	541	330	149	10	2
Private universities											
Humanities	0	15	71	152	182	138	142	111	60	0	0
Social sciences	2	21	95	167	165	132	133	94	63	0	0
Natural sciences	5	38	123	147	151	147	123	117	51	0	0
Total	7	74	289	466	498	417	398	322	174	0	0

TABLE 3-9

Distribution of Inflows and Gross Retention Rates among
Tenured Faculty by Age and Capping Status (percent)

Age Group	Capped Institutions		Uncapped Institutions	
	Distribution of Inflows	Retention Rates	Distribution of Inflows	Retention Rates
21–25	0.1	100.0	0.0	0.0
26–30	2.0	99.1	1.8	100.0
31–35	25.3	92.3	30.4	95.7
36–40	37.0	87.8	36.7	91.7
41–45	20.2	89.5	18.5	90.0
46–50	8.6	91.1	6.6	93.3
51–55	4.1	92.7	3.6	93.3
56–60	2.1	88.4	1.5	87.7
61–65	0.4	60.4	0.9	46.7
66–70	0.3	0.0	0.0	12.2
71–75	0.0	0.0	0.0	33.3
76–80	0.0	0.0	0.0	0.0

Net five-year percent change in tenured faculty
3.6   3.6

TABLE 3-10

Distribution of Inflows and Gross Retention Rates among Tenured Faculty by Age
and Institutional Type (percent)

Age Group	Private Universities		Public Universities		Liberal Arts Colleges	
	Distribution of Inflows	Retention Rates	Distribution of Inflows	Retention Rates	Distribution of Inflows	Retention Rates
21–25	0.2	100.0	0.0	0.0	0.0	0.0
26–30	3.0	100.0	1.4	97.1	0.8	100.0
31–35	26.8	90.1	25.1	100.0	28.9	92.7
36–40	35.5	88.1	37.1	98.8	39.9	88.9
41–45	17.9	89.0	20.9	92.3	21.7	89.1
46–50	8.8	90.8	8.3	92.9	6.3	92.1
51–55	5.0	92.0	4.2	93.9	1.2	93.1
56–60	2.2	87.5	2.0	88.9	1.2	88.8
61–65	0.7	68.3	0.7	36.4	0.0	55.6
66–70	0.2	0.0	0.3	2.1	0.0	4.8
71–75	0.0	0.0	0.0	0.0	0.0	22.2
76–80	0.0	0.0	0.0	0.0	0.0	0.0

Net five-year percent change in tenured faculty
4.1   2.7   5.0

TABLE 3-11

Inflows, Outflows, and Cohort Populations among Tenured Faculty by Capping Status (number)

	Capped Institutions				Uncapped Institutions			
Age Group	Inflows	1988–1989 Outflows	Population	1983–1984 Estimated Population	Inflows	1988–1989 Outflows	Population	1983–1984 Estimated Population
21–25	1	0	0	8	0	0	0	0
26–30	22	1	9	108	6	0	0	44
31–35	282	21	129	272	102	6	50	138
36–40	413	68	533	559	123	19	234	229
41–45	225	89	904	844	62	33	333	329
46–50	96	71	980	801	22	21	358	314
51–55	46	61	826	837	12	21	315	314
56–60	23	77	822	666	5	21	305	171
61–65	5	190	612	480	3	73	155	137
66–70	3	345	295	343	0	72	67	82
71–75	0	14	1	14	0	4	10	6
76–80	0	0	0	0	0	1	2	1

TABLE 3-12
Inflows, Outflows, and Cohort Populations among Tenured Faculty by Institutional Type (number)

Age Group	Private Universities				Public Universities				Liberal Arts Colleges			
	Inflows	Outflows	1988–1989 Population	1983–1984 Estimated Population	Inflows	Outflows	1988–1989 Population	1983–1984 Estimated Population	Inflows	Outflows	1988–1989 Population	1983–1984 Estimated Population
21–25	1	0	0	6	0	0	0	0	0	0	0	0
26–30	18	0	7	56	8	0	2	61	2	1	0	35
31–35	162	14	74	141	149	13	69	178	73	0	36	91
36–40	215	34	289	285	220	39	314	350	101	14	164	153
41–45	108	48	466	438	124	59	531	540	55	15	240	195
46–50	53	37	498	401	49	40	605	504	16	15	235	210
51–55	30	32	417	400	25	38	513	554	3	12	211	197
56–60	13	44	398	353	12	40	541	358	3	14	188	126
61–65	4	79	322	249	4	116	330	261	0	68	115	107
66–70	1	211	174	210	2	159	149	167	0	47	39	48
71–75	0	3	0	3	0	7	10	9	0	8	1	8
76–80	0	0	0	0	0	1	2	1	0	0	0	0

(1) We assume that the tenured force remains constant at the levels prevailing during academic year 1988–1989.

(2) We assume that the tenured force grows at the rate we estimate for each category of institution for the five years preceding academic year 1988–1989.

Within each of these analyses, we consider three scenarios for each category of institution:

(1) We assume that the flow patterns (with respect to both inflows and outflows) we observe in the most recent five-year period will continue in that institutional type into the future—a pattern we label "no change."

(2) We assume that the flow patterns (with respect to both inflows and outflows) we observe in the most recent five-year period for all cohorts through age 65 will continue in that institutional type into the future but that retention rates in the 66-to-75 cohorts will change to 13.6 percent,[11] beginning in the 1994–1999 time period and continuing thereafter—a pattern we label "moderate aging."[12]

(3) We assume that the flow patterns (with respect to both inflows and outflows) we observe in the most recent five-year period for all cohorts through age 65 will continue in that institutional type into the future but that retention rates in the 66-to-75 cohorts will change to 20.4 percent,[13] beginning in the 1994–1999 time period and continuing thereafter—a pattern we label "sharp aging."

Summary statistics from the projections we derive with the Stanford model under the constant-level assumption are presented in Table 3-13; those for the continued-growth assumption are shown in Table 3-14. For the projected Ns, see Tables 3-15 and 3-16. We show these figures at five-year intervals, from the starting point of our data, academic year 1988–1989, through academic year 2003–2004 but recognize that the estimates at the most distant point in time are subject to the greatest uncertainty. Several key points emerge.

First, the average age of tenured faculty will rise between 1989 and 1994 for all categories of institution whether or not the tenured force remains constant or grows at its most recently observed pace. The increase will be larger if the tenured force remains constant in size. The increase will be largest in uncapped institutions and liberal arts colleges, which currently have the lowest average ages. In all instances, the effect of the "aging" assumption on average age is very small. Moreover, regardless of the assumption with respect to the "aging" of

45

TABLE 3-13
Projected Age Patterns for Constant Tenured Force

	No Change[a]			Moderate Aging[b]			Sharp Aging[c]		
	% 40 and Under	% over 70	Average Age	% 40 and Under	% over 70	Average Age	% 40 and Under	% over 70	Average Age
Capped institutions									
1989	13	0.02	50.0	13	0.02	50.0	13	0.02	50.0
1994	14	0.0	50.7	14	0.0	50.7	14	0.0	50.7
1999	18	0.0	50.6	17	1.0	50.9	17	1.5	51.1
2004	20	0.0	50.2	19	1.3	50.5	19	2.1	50.6
Uncapped institutions									
1989	16	0.7	49.0	16	0.7	49.0	16	0.7	49.0
1994	13	0.6	50.3	14	0.5	50.3	13	0.9	50.4
1999	18	0.7	50.6	18	0.6	50.6	18	1.0	50.7
2004	20	1.0	50.1	20	1.0	50.1	20	1.6	50.2
Private universities									
1989	14	0.0	50.0	14	0.0	50.0	14	0.0	50.0
1994	15	0.0	50.6	15	0.0	50.6	15	0.0	50.6
1999	19	0.0	50.5	18	1.1	50.9	18	1.7	51.1
2004	20	0.0	50.2	19	1.4	50.5	19	2.2	50.6
Public universities									
1989	13	0.4	50.0	13	0.4	50.0	13	0.4	50.0
1994	13	0.3	50.9	13	0.3	50.9	13	0.3	50.9
1999	17	0.4	51.0	17	0.8	51.2	17	1.3	51.3
2004	19	0.5	50.3	19	1.3	50.5	19	2.1	50.7
Liberal arts colleges									
1989	16	0.1	48.7	16	0.1	48.7	16	0.1	48.7
1994	14	0.1	49.8	14	0.1	49.8	14	0.1	49.8
1999	18	0.1	50.1	17	0.5	50.3	17	0.7	50.3
2004	20	0.1	49.7	19	0.7	49.9	19	1.1	50.0

Note: Assumes tenured force remains constant at the level prevailing in the 1988–1989 academic year.

[a] Assumes historical flow patterns (that is, hiring distribution and retention rates) will prevail in the future.

[b] Assumes historical flow patterns will prevail in the future with the exception of the 66–70 and 71–75 age cohorts, whose retention rates will change to 13.6 percent, beginning in the 1994–1999 time period and continuing thereafter for all categories except uncapped institutions. The change in retention rates for these age cohorts in uncapped institutions begins in the 1989–1994 time period and continues thereafter.

[c] Assumes historical flow patterns will prevail in the future with the exception of the 66–70 and 71–75 age cohorts, whose retention rates will change to 20.4 percent, beginning in the 1994–1999 time period and continuing thereafter for all categories except uncapped institutions. The change in retention rates for these age cohorts in uncapped institutions begins in the 1989–1994 time period and continues thereafter.

TABLE 3-14
Projected Age Patterns for Tenured Force Growing at Historical Pace

	No Change[a]			Moderate Aging[b]			Sharp Aging[c]		
	% 40 and Under	% over 70	Average Age	% 40 and Under	% over 70	Average Age	% 40 and Under	% over 70	Average Age
Capped institutions									
1989	13	0.02	50.0	13	0.02	50.0	13	0.02	50.0
1994	16	0.0	50.2	16	0.0	50.2	16	0.0	50.2
1999	20	0.0	49.9	20	0.9	50.2	19	1.4	50.4
2004	21	0.0	49.4	21	1.2	49.7	20	1.9	49.8
Uncapped institutions									
1989	16	0.7	49.0	16	0.7	49.0	16	0.7	49.0
1994	15	0.6	49.8	15	0.5	49.9	15	0.8	50.0
1999	20	0.6	49.9	20	0.6	49.9	20	0.9	50.0
2004	22	0.9	49.3	22	0.9	49.3	22	1.4	49.4
Private universities									
1989	14	0.0	50.0	14	0.0	50.0	14	0.0	50.0
1994	17	0.0	50.1	17	0.0	50.1	17	0.0	50.1
1999	21	0.0	49.8	20	1.0	50.1	20	1.6	50.3
2004	22	0.0	49.3	22	1.2	49.6	21	1.9	49.7
Public universities									
1989	13	0.4	50.0	13	0.4	50.0	13	0.4	50.0
1994	15	0.3	50.6	15	0.3	50.6	15	0.3	50.6
1999	19	0.3	50.4	18	0.8	50.6	18	1.2	50.8
2004	21	0.5	49.7	20	1.2	50.0	20	1.9	50.0
Liberal arts colleges									
1989	16	0.1	48.7	16	0.1	48.7	16	0.1	48.7
1994	17	0.1	49.3	17	0.1	49.3	17	0.1	49.3
1999	21	0.1	49.2	21	0.4	49.3	20	0.7	49.4
2004	22	0.1	48.7	22	0.6	48.8	22	1.0	48.9

Note: Assumes tenured force grows at the same rate as that estimated for the five-year period preceding academic year 1988–1989.

[a] Assumes historical flow patterns (that is, hiring distribution and retention rates) will prevail in the future.

[b] Assumes historical flow patterns will prevail in the future with the exception of the 66–70 and 71–75 age cohorts, whose retention rates will change to 13.6 percent, beginning in the 1994–1999 time period and continuing thereafter for all categories except uncapped institutions. The change in retention rates for these age cohorts in uncapped institutions begins in the 1989–1994 time period and continues thereafter.

[c] Assumes historical flow patterns will prevail in the future with the exception of the 66–70 and 71–75 age cohorts, whose retention rates will change to 20.4 percent, beginning in the 1994–1999 time period and continuing thereafter for all categories except uncapped institutions. The change in retention rates for these age cohorts in uncapped institutions begins in the 1989–1994 time period and continues thereafter.

TABLE 3-15
Key Projections for Constant Tenured Force (number of faculty)

	No Change			Moderate Aging			Sharp Aging		
	40 and Under	41–70	Over 70	40 and Under	41–70	Over 70	40 and Under	41–70	Over 70
Capped institutions									
1989	671	4,439	1	671	4,439	1	671	4,439	1
1994	741	4,372	0	741	4,372	0	741	4,372	0
1999	925	4,190	0	892	4,172	51	875	4,162	76
2004	1,000	4,118	0	973	4,076	67	954	4,053	107
Uncapped institutions									
1989	284	1,533	12	284	1,533	12	284	1,533	12
1994	245	1,571	11	247	1,570	11	243	1,569	16
1999	322	1,493	12	323	1,493	12	320	1,490	18
2004	372	1,436	18	372	1,438	18	368	1,431	29
Private universities									
1989	370	2,275	0	370	2,275	0	370	2,275	0
1994	399	2,248	0	399	2,248	0	399	2,248	0
1999	498	2,151	0	477	2,139	30	468	2,135	45
2004	533	2,118	0	517	2,094	37	507	2,084	58
Public universities									
1989	385	2,669	12	385	2,669	12	385	2,669	12
1994	409	2,647	9	409	2,647	9	409	2,647	9
1999	528	2,527	11	517	2,522	26	508	2,517	39
2004	594	2,459	15	581	2,445	40	570	2,432	63
Liberal arts colleges									
1989	200	1,028	1	200	1,028	1	200	1,028	1
1994	173	1,056	1	173	1,056	1	173	1,056	1
1999	216	1,013	1	213	1,011	6	211	1,011	9
2004	243	987	1	239	982	9	237	981	14

Note: For key assumptions, see notes to Table 3-13.

TABLE 3-16
Key Projections for Tenured Force Growing at Historical Pace (number of faculty)

	No Change			Moderate Aging			Sharp Aging		
	40 and Under	41–70	Over 70	40 and Under	41–70	Over 70	40 and Under	41–70	Over 70
Capped institutions									
1989	671	4,439	1	671	4,439	1	671	4,439	1
1994	861	4,438	0	861	4,438	0	861	4,438	0
1999	1,107	4,384	0	1,075	4,367	51	1,059	4,357	76
2004	1,210	4,481	0	1,184	4,443	68	1,166	4,419	107
Uncapped institutions									
1989	284	1,533	12	284	1,533	12	284	1,533	12
1994	291	1,592	11	292	1,592	10	288	1,591	16
1999	393	1,558	12	394	1,558	11	391	1,555	18
2004	453	1,563	18	452	1,564	18	449	1,558	29
Private universities									
1989	370	2,275	0	370	2,275	0	370	2,275	0
1994	469	2,283	0	469	2,283	0	469	2,283	0
1999	606	2,259	0	587	2,248	30	577	2,244	45
2004	660	2,324	0	645	2,305	33	636	2,291	58
Public universities									
1989	385	2,669	12	385	2,669	12	385	2,669	12
1994	462	2,677	9	462	2,677	9	462	2,677	9
1999	607	2,616	11	597	2,611	26	589	2,606	39
2004	683	2,623	15	672	2,609	40	663	2,596	63
Liberal arts colleges									
1989	200	1,028	1	200	1,028	1	200	1,028	1
1994	216	1,074	1	216	1,074	1	216	1,074	1
1999	282	1,074	1	279	1,072	6	276	1,071	9
2004	316	1,107	1	314	1,103	9	311	1,099	14

Note: For key assumptions, see notes to Table 3-14.

the active tenured faculty or to the growth in the overall tenured force, our estimates suggest that the average age of the tenured faculty will begin to decline again by the end of the projection period in all categories of institutions.

Second, the proportion of the active tenured faculty over the age of 70 will rise in uncapped institutions and in all other institutions under either moderate or sharp aging assumptions. The increase will be somewhat larger if the overall tenured force remains constant in size. It is important to emphasize that in all instances the proportion will be quite small; at most, under sharp aging and constant tenured force assumptions, the projected proportion of tenured faculty over the age of 70 in private universities will rise from 0% to 2.2% in 2004.

Third, the proportion of the active tenured faculty aged 40 or under will also rise by the end of the projection period for all categories of institutions and under all aging assumptions. The increase will be somewhat larger if the overall tenured force is also growing. We estimate that this proportion will be 19 percent or more by the end of the projection period. Thus, even under the most aggressive aging assumptions, the faculty age distribution will be more widely spread across age brackets than it is at present, and the most elderly faculty will be a very small proportion of the total tenured force.

NOTES

1. One institution, which was able to provide good data on retirements, was unable to provide information on the age distribution of its current tenured faculty in the same academic year as that of the data provided by the other participating institutions. A second institution provided data on the age distribution of its tenured faculty in the appropriate academic year in interval format rather than as individual ages. Therefore the age distributions of both were excluded from the analysis that follows.

2. Mathematically, this faculty planning model is a Markov chain model with feedback. (Two other types of faculty flow models also in use for planning purposes are simulation models and difference equation models.) The COHORT model is based on Lotus 1-2-3 and was written by Rick Biedenweg and Tom Keenan for use at Stanford University but is being made available through the Consortium on Financing Higher Education for use at any institution. For an explanation of the workings of this model, see *The Faculty COHORT Model User Manual* by Rick Biedenweg and Tom Keenan (copyright 1989).

3. For further information on this survey and an analysis of its overall find-

ings, see Carnegie Foundation for the Advancement of Teaching, *The Condition of the Professoriate: Attitudes and Trends*, Carnegie Foundation Technical Report (Princeton, 1989).

4. For ease of comparison, percentages and the actual headcounts associated with each distribution are displayed in separate tables.

5. For example, if we were to simulate a 10 percent increase in the tenured faculty in the social sciences in a research institution, we would require detailed probabilities for the source of each of these new faculty members—that is, hire with tenure or promote from within—and the probable age of each at entrance.

6. For further discussion of the nature and workings of different types of faculty-planning models, see Christopher H. Nevison, "Effects of Tenure and Retirement Policies on the College Faculty: A Case Study Using Computer Simulation," *Journal of Higher Education* 51, no. 2 (1980): 150–66; and James A. Feldt, "Markov Models and Reductions in Work Force," in *Applying Decision Support Systems in Higher Education*, edited by John Rohrbaugh and Anne Taylor McCartt, New Directions for Institutional Research no. 49 (San Francisco: Jossey-Bass, 1986), 29–42.

7. The model does not allow retention rates to be less than zero even though negative retention rates could occur if the outflows during a five-year period were greater than the starting population because the entire starting population as well as some (and possibly all) of the individuals who entered the cohort also left during the same five-year period.

8. Moreover, for several institutions, the data on flows into and out of tenure refer to a period of time ending the year before the data on the age distribution. Therefore, the best approximation to the changes that have occurred in the tenured faculty in the five years preceding academic year 1988–1989 is the information on the flows during the five most recent years.

9. Alternatively, we could use the five most recent years of flow data to "youthen" the current tenured faculty in order to reconstruct the faculty age distribution of five years ago and derive the change in faculty size over the period. For example, to reconstruct tenured faculty of five years ago in the 41-to-45 age cohort from current tenured faculty in the 46-to-50 age cohort, we could use the data on the inflows and outflows in the most recent year in the 46-to-50 age cohort, one year previous in the 45-to-49 age cohort, two years previous in the 44-to-48 age cohort, three years previous in the 43-to-47 age cohort, and four years previous in the 42-to-46 age cohort. Although this technique has a certain intuitive appeal, it also has serious problems. Of the two techniques, it is more sensitive to errors in the original data gathered (for example, missing data on flows, errors in ages reported of either flows or the current stock, etc.) and to mismatches between the years of flow data reported and those needed to reconstruct the stock of tenured faculty five years ago. Moreover, this procedure, to some extent, treats the age cohorts in the 1988–1989 academic year as unique subsets. Accordingly, the determining factor in flow

patterns becomes the particular age cohort to which an individual would belong in 1988–1989.

10. This decline in the 61-to-65 age cohort could in part be the result of early retirement options, which would reduce the possibility of individuals remaining to age 70 or later.

11. This represents a weighted average of the retention rates observed in these cohorts in uncapped institutions.

12. The assumption that this change will begin in this time period is based on the assumption that no other institution will uncap before federal law so requires. In order to smooth the irregularities estimated in these age cohorts for uncapped institutions, the weighted average retention rate is also applied to these institutions, but beginning in the 1989–1994 time period because these institutions are already uncapped.

13. This represents a 50 percent increment in the weighted average of the retention rates observed in these age cohorts in currently uncapped institutions.

CHAPTER FOUR

Age and Faculty Productivity

IN THIS chapter, we examine the question of age and faculty vitality or productivity through a review of both the literature on this topic and the findings of several case studies on the subject that we have sponsored. Most research in this area addresses measures of performance, or outputs. We also include in our analysis some consideration of measures of effort, or inputs. The question of whether or not faculty performance deteriorates with age is really at the heart of the debate pertaining to the potential hazards of uncapping, for if faculty effectiveness continues unabated with age or even improves, one major cause of concern is removed.

The expectation that age is inevitably accompanied by a decline in performance and effectiveness is, in fact, the rationale underlying age discrimination. It should be emphasized that such discrimination may be directed against individuals who were highly valued at a younger age. DiGiovanni (1989) has observed that age discrimination is thus unique because it is not directed against the employee "because of who the worker *is*" but instead affects individuals because of "what they have *become*" (p. 2).

Mandatory retirement has often been viewed as a "humane" means to allow individuals to exit gracefully and avoid the indignity of exposing their anticipated loss of proficiency with age. Its elimination argues that age and effectiveness are not necessarily linked and that assessments of competence must be made on an individual basis. In the case of tenured faculty, the elimination of mandatory retirement also changes the meaning of tenure. The American Association of University Professors (1989) has suggested that with uncapping, tenure

> means that faculty members have tenure until *they* choose to retire, absent cause for dismissal or financial exigency. But it means, moreover, that by law their terms and conditions of employment cannot be different, because of their age, from those of their younger colleagues.

Implicit in this concern over faculty performance in an uncapped environment is, of course, the recognition that individual and institutional vitality are strongly correlated. The concept of "vitality" is itself somewhat nebulous. Drawing on the literature in this area, Clark, Boyer, and Corcoran (1985) have suggested that it be defined as "those essential, yet intangible, positive qualities of individuals and institutions that enable purposeful production" (p. 3). Indeed, the Planning Council of the University of Minnesota has defined a "vital" faculty as one that "exhibits sustained productivity in its teaching, its research, and its service activities."[1]

This definition highlights the fact that faculty are engaged in a number of very different activities in the academic community. Bowen and Schuster (1986, 14–24) have suggested that all of these can be divided into four overlapping tasks: teaching, research, institutional governance, and citizenship. The portion of time devoted to each of these functions varies substantially by type of institution. These differences, in turn, have implications for the concept of faculty vitality, since, as Clark, Boyer, and Corcoran (1985) have observed, "notions of faculty vitality seem to have a situational, contextual dimension that makes defining the concept difficult at best without taking into account institutional type and mission" (p. 10).

At issue here is whether changes in faculty performance in each of these principal functions can be anticipated as a consequence of age—whether inevitable or otherwise—and become especially troublesome past the age of 70. This analysis is not intended to deny the existence of individual differences, but rather to identify the areas where problems might be expected to occur if faculty choose to remain indefinitely and how these might differ by discipline, institutional type, and institutional mission.

FACULTY WORK EFFORT

To place this analysis in the appropriate institutional context, we will first direct our attention to the measures of faculty effort to see if and how these differ by institutional type and/or age cohort. The measure we use is the average of the approximate number of hours per week that tenured faculty in the arts and sciences report spending on ten different work activities. The data are drawn from the computer tape containing the 1989 National Survey of Faculty conducted for the Carnegie Foundation for the Advancement of Teaching.[2] Our sample of all tenured faculty in the arts and sciences in four-year institutions amounts to 2,005 individuals. We tabulate the responses to the ques-

TABLE 4-1
Hours Spent per Week by Tenured Faculty in Principal Functions
by Carnegie Classification

Carnegie Classification	Function					
	Teaching	Research	Admin.	Other	Total[a]	N
Number of Hours Spent per Week						
Research	20.4	20.5	7.5	1.5	49.9	526
Doctoral	25.2	14.5	7.2	1.6	48.5	535
Comprehensive	31.5	8.7	6.4	1.3	47.9	486
Liberal arts	29.3	9.8	5.9	1.2	46.2	455
Percent of Hours Spent per Week						
Research	40.9	41.1	15.0	3.0	100.0	526
Doctoral	52.0	29.9	14.8	3.3	100.0	535
Comprehensive	65.8	18.2	13.4	2.7	100.0	486
Liberal arts	63.4	21.2	12.8	2.6	100.0	455

Source: 1989 National Survey of Faculty, conducted for the Carnegie Foundation for the Advancement of Teaching (computer tape).

[a] Subcategories may not sum to total because of rounding.

tion "During this Spring term, approximately how many *hours per week* are you spending on each of the following activities?" to obtain average hours worked per week on the tasks of teaching, research, administration, and other, as well as total hours worked.[3] We then differentiate responses by broad Carnegie classification and by age cohort; the average number of hours worked and the distribution of the averages by function are displayed in Table 4-1.

Consistent with what has been observed in other studies, the time spent on each task varies substantially by type of institution. The differences are most marked for research and teaching and between research universities, where research is most important, and comprehensive institutions and liberal arts colleges, which emphasize teaching. There is far less variation in the total hours worked by Carnegie classification: It appears that tenured faculty members in this sample expend remarkably similar work effort, as measured by the total number of hours a week they report working, but they make that effort in very different ways.[4] For example, tenured faculty in all Carnegie classifications spend more than 80 percent of their time either in teaching and research. However, in research universities, faculty tend to divide that time equally between the two functions, whereas in liberal arts col-

TABLE 4-2

Hours Spent per Week by Tenured Faculty in Principal Functions by Carnegie Classification and Age Cohort

Age Group	Function					
	Teaching	Research	Admin.	Other	Total[a]	N
Research Universities						
Under 31	—	—	—	—	—	—
31–35	19.8	16.6	7.4	0.0	43.8	9
36–40	19.3	23.6	5.5	1.6	49.9	60
41–45	19.9	21.6	9.1	1.7	52.2	96
46–50	19.5	19.1	8.9	1.8	49.3	113
51–55	21.0	19.8	6.2	1.4	48.4	89
56–60	20.3	20.5	7.0	1.4	49.2	77
61–65	21.6	20.6	7.4	1.6	51.1	53
66–70	26.0	19.6	5.0	0.8	51.4	25
Over 70	15.3	12.5	14.0	0.3	42.0	4
Doctoral Institutions						
Under 31	23.0	20.0	0.0	0.0	43.0	1
31–35	20.2	22.6	2.0	0.8	45.6	5
36–40	25.8	16.2	6.8	1.7	50.5	38
41–45	22.2	14.8	7.6	1.7	46.2	59
46–50	25.6	15.8	8.3	1.7	51.4	148
51–55	26.2	12.7	7.2	1.6	47.8	114
56–60	25.3	13.6	7.2	2.0	48.2	95
61–65	24.9	13.1	6.1	1.0	45.2	50
66–70	26.5	16.1	3.7	0.5	46.8	24
Over 70	23.0	4.0	1.0	0.0	28.0	1
Comprehensive Institutions						
Under 31	—	—	—	—	—	—
31–35	34.5	5.5	5.8	1.5	47.3	4
36–40	32.3	13.0	4.4	1.0	50.7	36
41–45	30.4	8.9	7.1	1.5	47.9	83
46–50	29.9	9.7	8.8	1.8	50.1	121
51–55	30.9	7.0	7.6	1.1	46.5	89
56–60	33.7	8.0	4.4	1.1	47.1	91
61–65	33.9	7.8	4.2	0.5	46.4	47
66–70	31.4	6.7	2.1	1.5	41.7	13
Over 70	27.0	3.5	0.0	1.0	31.5	2

TABLE 4-2 (cont.)

Age Group	Function					
	Teaching	Research	Admin.	Other	Total[a]	N
	Liberal Arts Colleges					
Under 31	33.0	8.0	7.0	1.0	49.0	1
31–35	18.4	9.4	2.4	3.6	33.8	5
36–40	27.2	10.1	7.2	1.0	45.5	53
41–45	28.0	10.3	6.3	0.6	45.1	81
46–50	31.4	9.0	6.5	1.2	48.2	93
51–55	28.9	11.3	5.6	1.6	47.5	84
56–60	33.9	8.9	6.1	1.1	50.0	73
61–65	27.1	10.2	4.6	1.9	43.8	39
66–70	25.3	6.6	3.5	1.0	36.5	23
Over 70	8.0	16.7	0.0	0.7	25.3	3

Source: Same as Table 4-1.
[a] Subcategories may not sum to total because of rounding.

leges, faculty spend three-quarters or more of that time teaching. These observations would thus suggest that the areas of scrutiny in terms of maintaining faculty vitality will differ by institutional type. Teaching is clearly an area for concern in all institutions, but research has far more significance in research universities and doctoral institutions than elsewhere.

If we now look for differences by age cohort in work effort, we see remarkable similarity within Carnegie classifications across age cohorts from the early 30s through age 70. Table 4-2 displays the average hours by function, broad Carnegie classification, and age cohort; Table 4-3 shows the distribution of these averages. It is reassuring to observe that, at least up to the current mandatory retirement age, faculty continue to expend a similar quantity of work effort throughout their careers.[5] Although there are some faculty in this sample above age 70, the numbers are too small to draw any strong conclusions in this regard. However, given the uniformity observed throughout the earlier age groups, it seems highly unlikely that a dramatic change would occur among faculty who chose to remain active after age 70.

The remaining issue, then, is whether changes in the quality of the faculty effort can be anticipated with age and become especially troublesome past the age of 70. Because the importance of faculty functions differs by institutional type and because the means for assessing the

TABLE 4-3

Percentage of Hours Spent per Week by Tenured Faculty in Principal
Functions by Carnegie Classification and Age Cohort

Age Group	Function					
	Teaching	Research	Admin.	Other	Total[a]	N
Research Universities						
Under 31	—	—	—	—	—	—
31–35	45.2	37.9	16.9	0.0	100.0	9
36–40	38.7	47.3	11.0	3.2	100.0	60
41–45	38.1	41.4	17.4	3.3	100.0	96
46–50	39.6	38.7	18.1	3.7	100.0	113
51–55	43.4	40.9	12.8	2.9	100.0	89
56–60	41.3	41.7	14.2	2.8	100.0	77
61–65	42.3	40.3	14.5	3.1	100.0	53
66–70	50.6	38.1	9.7	1.6	100.0	25
Over 70	36.4	29.8	33.3	0.7	100.0	4
Doctoral Institutions						
Under 31	53.5	46.5	0.0	0.0	100.0	1
31–35	44.3	49.6	4.4	1.8	100.0	5
36–40	51.1	32.1	13.5	3.4	100.0	38
41–45	48.1	32.0	16.5	3.7	100.0	59
46–50	49.8	30.7	16.1	3.3	100.0	148
51–55	54.8	26.6	15.1	3.3	100.0	114
56–60	52.5	28.2	14.9	4.1	100.0	95
61–65	55.1	29.0	13.5	2.2	100.0	50
66–70	56.6	34.4	7.9	1.1	100.0	24
Over 70	82.1	14.3	3.6	0.0	100.0	1
Comprehensive Institutions						
Under 31	—	—	—	—	—	—
31–35	72.9	11.6	12.3	3.2	100.0	4
36–40	63.7	25.6	8.7	2.0	100.0	36
41–45	63.5	18.6	14.8	3.1	100.0	83
46–50	59.7	19.4	17.6	3.6	100.0	121
51–55	66.5	15.1	16.3	2.4	100.0	89
56–60	71.5	17.0	9.3	2.3	100.0	91
61–65	73.1	16.8	9.1	1.1	100.0	47
66–70	75.3	16.1	5.0	3.6	100.0	13
Over 70	85.7	11.1	0.0	3.2	100.0	2

TABLE 4-3 (*cont.*)

Age Group	Function					
	Teaching	Research	Admin.	Other	Total[a]	N
Liberal Arts Colleges						
Under 31	67.3	16.3	14.3	2.0	100.0	1
31–35	54.4	27.8	7.1	10.7	100.0	5
36–40	59.8	22.2	15.8	2.2	100.0	53
41–45	62.1	22.8	14.0	1.3	100.0	81
46–50	65.1	18.7	13.5	2.5	100.0	93
51–55	60.8	23.8	11.8	3.4	100.0	84
56–60	67.8	17.8	12.2	2.2	100.0	73
61–65	61.9	23.3	10.5	4.3	100.0	39
66–70	69.3	18.1	9.6	2.7	100.0	23
Over 70	31.6	66.0	0.0	2.8	100.0	3

Source: Same as Table 4-1.

[a] Subcategories may not sum to total because of rounding.

quality of effort in each differs by function, this question will be considered separately for the two principal functions of research and teaching.

The third function to which faculty devote notable proportions of time is administration. Indeed, the observation that some faculty members report working on this task as much as sixty hours per week suggests that the sample includes some full-time administrators. If these administrators have bona fide policymaking powers, then, under the terms of the Age Discrimination in Employment Act (as enacted in 1967 and amended in 1978 and 1986), they can still be made subject to a mandatory retirement age of 65 from their administrative posts but not from their tenured faculty positions.[6] Thus, the relationship between age and administrative effectiveness is not a question that calls for further attention in this study.

TEACHING EFFECTIVENESS

There is a large body of research on the evaluation of teaching effectiveness.[7] In general, it falls into two broad topics: identification of the individual characteristics connected with good teaching and analysis of the relative merits of different teaching methods. Accordingly, the findings have been used not only to advance knowledge but also to improve faculty performance and to guide personnel decisions. For our purposes, what is of interest is an analysis of the characteristics of the teacher that are associated with "good teaching"—in particular, whether age is a contributing factor or a hindrance in this regard. We have sponsored one case study examining this question in a single private Research I institution.[8] We will summarize the findings of this study and also discuss certain other information we obtained on this question while we were collecting our main body of data.

There are a number of measures in use to assess teaching effectiveness. Of these, systematic student ratings are one of the ones used most often at both public and private liberal arts colleges and research and comprehensive universities.[9] Empirical studies in this area confirm the reliability and stability of student ratings in assessing teaching competence, though these studies have also identified a number of factors that influence student ratings but which are beyond the control of the instructor.[10]

The case study we sponsored (Kinney and Smith [1989]) adds to this literature by focusing on the relationship between faculty age and student evaluation of overall teaching effectiveness and the relationship between teaching effectiveness and the timing of the retirement decision (that is, retiring at the mandatory age or "early"). The study used two data sets: one pertaining to the summary student evaluations of the overall quality of teaching in courses taught during the five-year period ending in academic year 1986–1987 by faculty who were tenured as of academic year 1987–1988 in the arts and sciences in a single private Research I university;[11] and the second pertaining to the summary student evaluations of the overall quality of teaching in each of the courses taught during the period academic year 1971–1972 through academic year 1987–1988 by the tenured faculty members who also retired during that time frame. This institution currently maintains a policy for its tenured faculty of mandatory retirement at age 70. Separate equations were then estimated for each of the three broad discipline categories—humanities, social sciences, and physical and biological sciences.

The forms used to collect evaluation information from the students at this institution are distributed in each course, generally in the last two weeks of each semester. Students are asked to provide a comprehensive rating of the "overall quality of teaching in the course." In addition, students are asked to assess such separate aspects of the course and the teacher as the quality and relative value of lectures, readings, discussion groups, papers, reports, and problem sets. Each of the questions is answered on a five-point scale, with 1 = "unacceptable," 2 = "poor," 3 = "fair," 4 = "good," and 5 = "excellent" (and 0 = "not applicable"). Summary data are available for each course on the number of students in the course, the number of respondents to the form, and the average student rating for each question on the form.

Regressions were estimated, with use of a variety of functional forms, for the relationships between student evaluations and characteristics of the course (such as level and class size), of the instructor (such as age), and of the student (such as prior interest, which can be proxied with information on whether or not the class is required). The results for the best fit for each discipline are displayed in Table 4-4.[12] "Corrected" refers to the White (1980) correction for heteroscedasticity. This study suggested that there is a significant, curvilinear relationship between teaching effectiveness and age among the active tenured faculty and that the relationship varies structurally across the broad discipline categories.

These findings are summarized in Figure 4-1 (reproduced from Kinney and Smith [1989]), which displays the student evaluations estimated by the best model for each discipline at each age from 35 to 70 (evaluated at the mean level in each discipline for each of the other explanatory variables). In general, evaluations tend to be highest in the humanities and lowest in the physical and biological sciences. It appears that student evaluations of teaching effectiveness actually improve for tenured professors in the humanities and the social sciences as they approach the current mandatory retirement age, though in the social sciences, these evaluations first decline between the early 40s and the mid-60s. It is only in the physical and biological sciences that student evaluations of teaching effectiveness decline as faculty approach the current mandatory retirement age. In each discipline, however, the impact of age on these evaluations of teaching effectiveness is very small in size. If we use these results to extrapolate beyond age 70, they suggest that if a tenured professor were to work one additional year, his or her teaching rating would rise by 0.02 points (on a scale of 5 points) in either the humanities or the social sciences and would fall by 0.06 points in the physical and biological sciences. In contrast, a course taught at the highest level in the social sciences would have an

TABLE 4-4

Teaching Effectiveness in a Research I University—Results of Regressions

Variable	Coefficient	Standard Error	Corrected	Variable Mean	Variable Standard Error
Humanities[a]					
Constant	5.553	0.440	0.377**	1.00	0.00
AGE	−0.051	0.018	0.016**	47.88	8.76
AGE^2	0.001	0.0002	0.0002**	2,368.79	834.82
REQUIRED	−0.052	0.055	0.053	0.20	0.40
SHARED	−0.209	0.054	0.060**	0.10	0.30
LOWLEVEL	−0.064	0.067	0.067	0.28	0.45
MIDLEVEL	0.078	0.069	0.061	0.52	0.50
UPPERLEVEL	0.045	0.095	0.097	0.06	0.24
SMALLENR	0.134	0.035	0.036**	0.44	0.50
LARGEENR	0.065	0.062	0.061	0.08	0.27
RATING				4.37	0.43
Social sciences[b]					
Constant	−0.783	2.123	2.071	1.00	0.00
AGE	0.293	0.139	0.135*	47.69	10.18
AGE^2	−0.006	0.003	0.003*	2,378.00	981.08
AGE^3	0.00004	0.00002	0.00002	123,322.56	73,726.02
REQUIRED	−0.187	0.071	0.070**	0.17	0.37
SHARED	0.087	0.062	0.051*	0.15	0.36
LOWLEVEL	0.251	0.107	0.095**	0.20	0.40
MIDLEVEL	0.465	0.105	0.097**	0.66	0.47
UPPERLEVEL	0.803	0.140	0.130**	0.06	0.24
SMALLENR	−0.026	0.056	0.063	0.20	0.40
LARGEENR	0.022	0.052	0.043	0.26	0.44
RATING				4.25	0.45
Physical and biological sciences[c]					
Constant	1.537	0.601	0.623*	1.00	0.00
AGE	0.117	0.025	0.027**	46.91	10.35
AGE^2	−0.001	0.0003	0.0003**	2,307.00	987.03
REQUIRED	−0.210	0.061	0.064**	0.42	0.49
SHARED	−0.102	0.071	0.074	0.18	0.38
LOWLEVEL	−0.212	0.097	0.084*	0.20	0.40
MIDLEVEL	−0.023	0.100	0.085	0.39	0.49
UPPERLEVEL	0.150	0.113	0.103	0.31	0.46
SMALLENR	0.088	0.059	0.063	0.36	0.48
LARGEENR	−0.036	0.075	0.072	0.23	0.42
RATING				3.99	0.56

Source: Kinney and Smith 1989.

[a] $N = 664$; $R^2 = 0.101$; adjusted $R^2 = 0.089$.

[b] $N = 404$; $R^2 = 0.215$; adjusted $R^2 = 0.195$.

[c] $N = 455$; $R^2 = 0.184$; adjusted $R^2 = 0.168$.

* Significant at the 0.05 level.

** Significant at the 0.01 level.

FIGURE 4-1

Teaching Effectiveness by Age and Broad Discipline Category among
Tenured Faculty at a Research I University: Best Fit Evaluated at Means

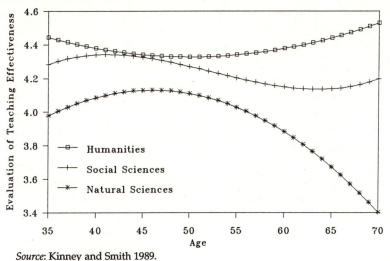

Source: Kinney and Smith 1989.

evaluation a full 0.8 points higher than that of a course taught at the
lowest level. Similarly, a required course in the physical and biological
sciences would have an evaluation 0.2 points lower than that of an
elective.

The analysis of the relationship between teaching effectiveness and
the timing of the retirement decision also shows that the patterns differ
by discipline. The model that had provided the best fit in the previous
analysis was reestimated with use of the evaluation data for retirees.[13]
The results are somewhat mixed. The age variables lose significance in
all models except that for the physical and biological sciences. This loss
in significance is not surprising, however, given that the influence of
age on teaching effectiveness at later ages was shown to be of very
small size.

There appears to be adverse self-selection in both the humanities and
the physical and biological sciences in the sense that the more effective
teachers retire early. This suggests that the remaining pool of professors in these two disciplines will be of lower average teaching effectiveness. In the humanities, the model suggests that courses taught by
those who retire at the mandatory age tend to be rated 0.19 points
below those taught by professors who choose to retire early, and this
effect is significant at the 1 percent level. In the physical and biological

sciences, negative self-selection is also suggested, but the estimated effect is not significant. In the social sciences, in contrast, there is favorable self-selection, as the less effective teachers choose to retire early; the estimated difference is 0.21 points and is significant at the 5 percent level.

When the findings of these two analyses are viewed together, it appears that the impending uncapping of retirement for tenured faculty raises no major concerns for dramatic deterioration in teaching effectiveness in an aging professoriat. Some problems might ultimately occur in the physical and biological sciences, where a slight decline in student evaluations of teaching effectiveness with age is compounded with possible adverse self-selection such that the teachers who are rated as more effective seem to decide to retire early, thus leaving a remaining pool of faculty of even lower average teaching effectiveness. Even compounded, these effects are quite small, but will probably become larger if retirement is postponed indefinitely beyond the current mandatory retirement age. At the same time, however, it should be emphasized that these findings are based on a relatively small data set pertaining to only one institution. Thus, while we view them as suggestive, they may not be generalizable.

To probe this point further, we sought similar data on the teaching effectiveness of tenured faculty in other institutions. Although many institutions have student evaluation systems in place, few are comparable to the institution Kinney and Smith analyzed. Many allow evaluation forms to be distributed at the discretion of the professor. Many do not retain the evaluation data they collect. Others view the data as confidential and cannot share it with researchers.

One institution—a private Research II university—did have comparable evaluation data, as well as information on some of the other explanatory variables used in the Kinney and Smith analysis.[14] This institution also has a policy of mandatory retirement for its tenured faculty at age 70. Using these data, we estimated various functional forms. The results for the best fit for each discipline are displayed in Table 4-5. The results again show a significant relationship between student evaluations of teaching effectiveness and age, which varies structurally across the discipline categories.[15] These findings are summarized in Figure 4-2, which, like Figure 4-1, displays the student evaluations estimated by the best model for each discipline at each age from 35 to 70 (evaluated at the mean level in each discipline for each of the other explanatory variables).

TABLE 4-5
Teaching Effectiveness in a Research II
University—Results of Regressions

Variable	Coefficient	Standard Error
Humanities[a]		
Constant	3.326***	0.525
AGE	0.053***	0.020
AGE^2	−0.0006***	0.0002
LOWLEVEL	−0.063*	0.037
MIDLEVEL	−0.065	0.042
UPPERLEVEL	0.125**	0.052
SMALLENR	0.022	0.035
LARGEENR	−0.113	0.323
Social sciences[b]		
Constant	−0.783	2.921
AGE	0.337*	0.178
AGE^2	−0.007**	0.004
AGE^3	0.00005**	0.00002
LOWLEVEL	0.168***	0.061
MIDLEVEL	0.146***	0.050
UPPERLEVEL	0.341***	0.059
SMALLENR	0.055	0.043
LARGEENR	0.206**	0.094
Physical and biological sciences[c]		
Constant	4.130***	0.202
AGE	−0.006	0.004
LOWLEVEL	0.317***	0.081
MIDLEVEL	0.295***	0.086
UPPERLEVEL	0.739***	0.228
SMALLENR	0.020	0.081
LARGEENR	0.135	0.314

[a] $N = 997$; $R^2 = 0.082$; adjusted $R^2 = 0.075$.
[b] $N = 827$; $R^2 = 0.097$; adjusted $R^2 = 0.088$.
[c] $N = 387$; $R^2 = 0.092$; adjusted $R^2 = 0.077$.
* Significant at the 0.10 level.
** Significant at the 0.05 level.
*** Significant at the 0.01 level.

FIGURE 4-2

Teaching Effectiveness by Age and Broad Discipline Category among
Tenured Faculty at a Research II University: Best Fit Evaluated at Means

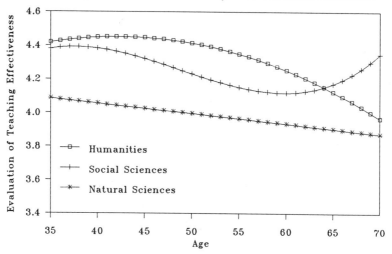

The impact of age is again quite small in size. Consistent with the findings of Kinney and Smith for a private Research I university (RU1), evaluations in this private Research II university (RU2) tend to be highest in the humanities (at least before age 60) and lowest in the physical and biological sciences, though the distinctions are not so marked. The estimated shapes of the relationships also differ somewhat from those estimated for RU1. For example, whereas the social sciences again show a pattern of improving evaluations of teaching effectiveness for those over age 60, the humanities do not. Although the physical and biological sciences show a pattern of linear decline in the evaluations with age, it should be emphasized that the relationship here is weak. If we use these results to extrapolate beyond age 70, they suggest that if a tenured professor were to work one additional year, the teaching rating would fall by 0.04 points (on a scale of 5 points) in the humanities, rise by 0.002 points in the social sciences, and fall by 0.006 points in the physical and biological sciences. Thus, these results also suggest that uncapping presents no major concerns for a striking deterioration in the quality of teaching with an aging professoriat.

One other institution—a Liberal Arts I college—provided us with some additional information concerning the relationship between teaching effectiveness and the timing of the retirement decision. This institution, like the two research universities, is still capped. Its data, unlike those for the research universities, are based on assessments and rankings by the provost and dean of the faculty, not on student evaluations. These rankings suggest that "there is almost no discernible difference" between the early retirees (that is, ages 62–66) and the late and/or mandatory retirees (that is, ages 68–70) in terms of their teaching. It should also be noted that a relatively small proportion (four out of thirty-one) of the retirees in general were viewed as inferior teachers—which may reflect generally satisfactory teaching among older faculty at this institution. These findings should again be viewed only as suggestive, as the number of retirees in question is small, the rankings are judgmental, and significance tests are not possible.

Nevertheless, these data provide some additional support to the picture that is emerging. It appears likely that in an uncapped world, if some faculty do remain beyond the current mandatory retirement age, there will be some decline in teaching effectiveness among aging professors, but it will be quite small in size and not uniform across discipline categories. Indeed, some disciplines will see an improvement in teaching effectiveness among aging faculty. At the same time, however, it appears that relative teaching effectiveness also enters into the timing of the retirement decision, though this pattern is also strongly affected by institutional type.

RESEARCH OUTPUT

When we turn to the relationship between research activity and age, we focus on the function that defines distinguished universities.[16] As we have already seen, it is these institutions where uncapping of the faculty retirement age is anticipated to have the greatest behavioral impact. There is a large literature addressing the issue of research activity from a variety of perspectives (of which the age profile is only one aspect).[17] This research suggests that the relationship is generally curvilinear, though the shape of the curve varies by discipline and by measure of research performance. The effect of aging by itself again appears to be fairly small. Other factors, which may be partially linked to age—such as cohort and market effects—also influence performance, and the separate influence of each may be difficult to disentangle.

Recent research by Stephan and Levin (1987) suggests that the productivity of scientists varies by the "vintage" of their training and may compound the effect of aging. They conclude that

> as the scientific community ages and members of the earlier cohorts retire, other things being equal, the mean level of publishing productivity will also decline. Thus the American scientific community of the next thirty years may not be as productive as a younger community was in the 1960's and 1970's for two reasons: age per se and the retirement of the more productive, earlier cohorts. (p. iv)

We will summarize the findings of a case study we sponsored and also report on other information gathered from the institutions participating in our sample. We are able to add to the existing literature because we analyze data sources not previously used for this purpose.

Many measures have been used to assess research and scholarship, including number of publications (sometimes weighted with respect to either the length or the quality of the publication), number of citations to publications, attitudes toward research, time spent in research, receipt of outside support, and volume and type of outside support received.[18] Each of these has its own advantages and disadvantages. Moreover, standards and practice with respect to each of the activities accounted for by these measures vary by institutional type and discipline.

Howe and Smith (1991) used three data sets from two sources to assess the relationship between age and research activity: data on the number of publications in the last two years and on the receipt of support in a major grant—defined as a grant from a federal agency, a foundation, or private industry—within the last twelve months were obtained from the extract from the Carnegie survey (described above);[19] and data on the receipt of support in major grants and the dollar amount of that support received over a five-year period were drawn from the records on research and project administration for tenured faculty in the social sciences and the physical and biological sciences at one private Research I university.[20]

This study indicated that the relationship between age and recent publications differs markedly by discipline. For both the humanities and the physical and biological sciences, the best-fitting specification suggests a leveling-out relationship in which the effect of age on research activity plateaus. In contrast, the best-fitting specification for the social sciences suggests a linear relationship. These results, which are

TABLE 4-6
Determinants of Publishing Activity

	Humanities		Social Sciences		Physical and Biological Sciences	
	Coeff.	t-Stat.	Coeff.	t-Stat.	Coeff.	t-Stat.
Constant	0.93	1.34	5.95	7.68	−0.65	−0.59
AGE	—	—	−0.053	−3.58	—	—
1/AGE	85.48	2.65	—	—	184.07	3.82
FEMALE	−0.77	−3.17	−0.26	−0.85	−1.12	−2.18
RESEARCH	1.08	3.54	1.14	3.05	2.62	5.31
DOCTORAL	0.57	1.94	0.26	0.73	0.67	1.39
COMPREHENSIVE	0.00	0.00	−0.83	−2.25	−0.35	−0.70
PRTEACH	−1.84	−7.60	−2.11	−6.47	−2.22	−5.54
PRRESEARCH	0.97	2.04	2.10	5.02	3.70	6.96
Adjusted R^2	0.15		0.24		0.33	
N	(778)		(565)		(562)	

Source: Howe and Smith 1991.
Note: Dependent variable is RECENTPUB.

displayed in Table 4-6, indicate that current research activity (as measured by recent publications) decreases in each of the three discipline categories as tenured faculty age. However, the largest decline occurs long before the individual approaches the current mandatory retirement age of 70.

These findings are summarized in Figure 4-3 (reproduced from Howe and Smith [1991]), which displays recent publications forecast by the best model for each discipline at each age from 35 to 70 (evaluated at the mean level in each discipline for each of the other explanatory variables).[21] They show that between age 60 and age 70, recent publishing activity for the average tenured faculty member would decrease by 0.2 articles in the humanities, by 0.5 articles in the social sciences, and by 0.4 articles in the physical and biological sciences.

It should be noted that these results do not suggest that research activity ceases as the faculty member approaches the current mandatory retirement age. Even in the least active discipline—the humanities—these forecasts suggest that the average tenured faculty member would still be producing nearly 2 publications every two years at age 70, whereas in the most active discipline—the physical and biological

FIGURE 4-3

Research Activity of Tenured Faculty by Age and Broad Discipline
Category: Best Fit Evaluated at Means

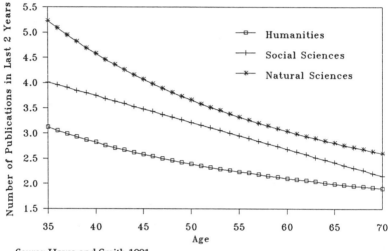

Source: Howe and Smith 1991.

sciences—the average faculty member would be producing 2.6 articles. Like the findings of Kinney and Smith, these results suggest that other factors than age have a much larger influence on publishing activity. For example, being in a research university increases the publishing activity of the average tenured faculty member in the physical and biological sciences by 2.6 articles, as compared with a similar tenured faculty member in the liberal arts colleges.

Several individual institutions provided a variety of data concerning the publishing activity of their tenured faculty. For example, a Liberal Arts I college (the one discussed above in the analysis of teaching effectiveness) offered an assessment and ranking by the provost and dean of the faculty of the "scholarship" of its retirees. Differences do emerge here between early and late/mandatory retirees. It appears that at this institution the "early retirement cohort in general outperformed the late retirement quite substantially in respect to scholarship." At the same time, it seems that there was about the same proportion of "underachievers" in both groups.

It is possible that the superior researchers here retired early in order to engage in their research full time, since this institution provides its retired faculty with a fairly full array of benefits and privileges. These include full library privileges; access to office and laboratory space (if possible); access to secretarial services (if time is available); computer support; and the opportunity to serve as principal investigator and to compete for research funds along with the active faculty.

Research currently under way at Barnard College into the scholarly activities of faculty in the humanities and the social sciences in liberal arts colleges provides further confirmation of the patterns observed in the Carnegie data.[22] In particular, this research shows that although faculty aged 50 and over are represented in the top quartile of number of publications commensurate with their representation in the population, faculty between the ages of 40 and 49 comprise a larger proportion of this top quartile than their proportion in the population. These results again suggest that research certainly continues in this older cohort but that some decline in activity has occurred relative to their younger colleagues.

The second measure of research activity analyzed by Howe and Smith—the acquisition of outside grants and the dollar value of the grants awarded—offers a somewhat different perspective on the relationship between age and research activity. On the one hand, these measures gauge not only continuing research activity but also the positive appraisal of the research abilities of the grantee. On the other hand, these measures, unlike the number of publications, may also be affected by age discrimination on the part of the grantor, since the refereeing of publications is often "blind" whereas the refereeing of grant applications is not.

Thus there may be a decline with age in the probability of receiving grant support and/or in the dollars received for two reasons: Older faculty may be less active researchers, and organizations awarding grants may discriminate against older investigators. Because the information in both data sets pertains to grants awarded, not grant applications, it is difficult to gauge the magnitude of this potential bias. However, a recent study showing that the average age of investigators at both the Alcohol, Drug Abuse, and Mental Health Administration (ADAMHA) and the National Institute of Health (NIH) has been rising (see U.S. Department of Health and Human Services 1988) suggests that this bias, if present, is probably decreasing.

Estimates by Howe and Smith of the determinants of the receipt of major grant support for research activity show that there are again marked differences by discipline, with age showing a negative and significant but small effect.[23] These results are displayed in Table 4-7. At

TABLE 4-7

Probit Estimates of Determinants of Receipt of Major Grants

	Social Sciences			Physical and Biological Sciences		
	Coeff.	*t-Stat.*	$\delta P/\delta X^a$	*Coeff.*	*t-Stat.*	$\delta P/\delta X^a$
INTERCEPT	0.74	2.09		1.34	3.47	
AGE	–0.019	–2.73	–0.0065	–0.022	–3.01	–0.0086
FEMALE	–0.31	–2.16	–0.11	–0.32	–1.55	–0.13
RESEARCH	–0.12	–0.72	–0.042	0.37	2.00	0.15
DOCTORAL	–0.31	–1.92	–0.11	–0.22	–1.19	–0.088
COMPREHENSIVE	–0.51	–2.97	–0.18	–0.19	–1.00	–0.076
PRTEACH	–0.48	–2.93	–0.17	–1.34	–8.02	–0.53
PRRESEARCH	0.57	3.17	0.20	0.64	3.16	0.26
Mean of dependent variable	0.31			0.48		

	$\delta P/\delta X^b$	$\delta P/\delta X^b$
Selected Ages		
60	–0.0057	–0.0084
65	–0.0053	–0.0081
70	–0.0049	–0.0077
75	–0.0045	–0.0072

Source: Howe and Smith 1991.

Note: Dependent variable is HIGRANT. Sample size is 582 for social sciences and 583 for physical and biological sciences.

[a] Evaluated at the mean for all explanatory variables.

[b] Evaluated at selected ages and the mean values for all explanatory variables other than age.

the mean age for each discipline—49.4 for the social sciences and 51.9 for the physical and biological sciences—and at the mean levels for the other explanatory variables, an additional year of age would reduce the probability of receiving a major grant by 0.0065 in the social sciences and by 0.0086 in the physical and biological sciences. At age 70, these estimated marginal probabilities are 0.0049 and 0.0077 respectively. In contrast, being in a research university (as compared with a liberal arts college) increases the probability of receiving major grant support in the physical and biological sciences by 0.15.

Using these estimates to simulate the implications for successful grant getting in an aging professoriat, Howe and Smith demonstrated that a steady falloff in the success rate with age is likely. It appears that this success rate in obtaining major grant support is likely to be higher at every age in the physical and biological sciences, but the relative drop-off with age is somewhat less severe. At the same time, however, it is important to note that the Carnegie data clearly indicate that the oldest faculty do continue to obtain grant support.

Further evidence on these patterns can be found in Howe and Smith's second data source: the grant records from a single private Research I university over the five-year period ending in academic year 1988–1989, including grants that were completed before 1988–1989 and those still active during the year.[24] A weighting scheme was developed to assign grant dollars to primary and secondary investigators.[25]

When faculty are grouped into five-year cohorts within disciplines, a clear pattern emerges. Figure 4-4 shows the pattern for social sciences faculty; Figure 4-5 shows it for natural sciences faculty. For each cohort, these figures display grant dollars averaged over all tenured faculty in the cohort and grant dollars averaged only over those faculty members who had received grant support. The figures also show the proportion in the cohort who received support. For example, Figure 4-5 indicates that 57.1 percent of the tenured faculty in the 46-to-50 age cohort in the physical and biological sciences received major grant support at some time during this five-year period. This support amounted to an annual average of $449,000 per member of the cohort, or $800,000 each among those in the cohort who received grants.

A review of these data indicates that tenured faculty received major grant support in all age cohorts in both disciplines, although the absolute dollar amount of the grant support tends to be dramatically larger in the physical and biological sciences.[26] The study indicates that average grant dollars peaked around age 50[27] and that both the proportion of faculty in any age cohort who receive grant dollars and the average amount of those dollars declines with age after age 55 though the decline in dollars received was much more severe than in the proportion receiving support.

If these observations of declining amounts of grant support with faculty age are suggestive of the patterns for other institutions, they offer another indication of reduced research activity. However, the decline is clearly not an issue in the analysis of the impact of the elimination of

FIGURE 4-4

Average Annual Grant Dollars by Age among Social Sciences Tenured
Faculty at a Research I University

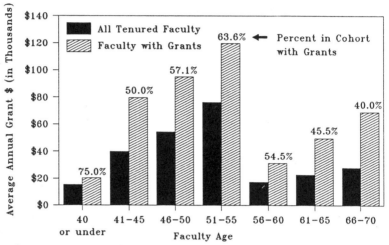

Source: Howe and Smith 1991.

FIGURE 4-5

Average Annual Grant Dollars by Age among Natural Sciences Tenured
Faculty at a Research I University

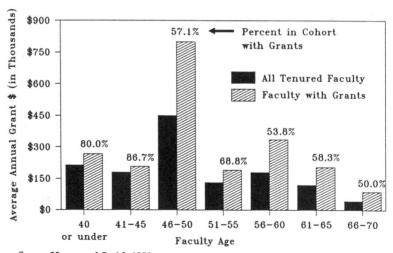

Source: Howe and Smith 1991.

mandatory retirement, for the most serious decrease occurs long before the current mandatory retirement age. There is, of course, one important qualification to this observation: If a threshold absolute level of outside funding is needed to support the research needs of faculty in the physical and biological sciences, then this pattern of precipitous decline may put an aging faculty in these disciplines at risk in this regard.

NOTES

1. Planning Council, University of Minnesota 1980, 4, as cited in Clark, Boyer, and Corcoran 1985, 10.

2. See Carnegie Foundation for the Advancement of Teaching, *The Condition of the Professoriate: Attitudes and Trends*, A Carnegie Foundation Technical Report, (Princeton, 1989), for an analysis of the findings of this survey.

3. Three individuals were omitted from the sample when we made these tabulations because of apparent coding errors (the individuals reported more hours at work than are available in a week). In particular, we include in the category "teaching" the following activities (as specified in the survey questionnaire): "formal classroom instruction in *undergraduate* courses (give actual, not credit hours)"; "formal classroom instruction in *graduate or professional* courses (give actual, not credit hours)"; "preparation for teaching"; "scheduled office hours"; "academic advising"; "service with co-curricular student activities"; and "supervising graduate teaching assistant." "Research" is the single task described as "research and/or comparable scholarly activities." "Administration" is also a single task described as "administrative service (departmental or institutional)." "Other" is the single task, described as "consulting (with or without pay)." It should be noted that because of rounding, the means for the subcategories will not total the mean for the total hours worked.

4. It is important to recognize that this measure is a very rough one, as it is a self-reported indication of time spent in specified activities and cannot take any account of the "quality" of the time spent or the consequences of the time spent in these activities. The twenty hours spent in research that results in a major breakthough in the discipline and many publications in first-rate journals cannot be distinguished from the twenty hours spent in research that produces no significant findings and yields no publications.

5. Of course, once again, we can make no assessment of the consequences of this effort.

6. This exemption is limited, since it permits mandatory retirement of such administrators only if they have been employed in a bona fide executive or

policymaking position for at least two years immediately prior to retirement and are entitled to an immediate, nonforfeitable retirement benefit (exclusive of contributions of their own or of other employers) of $27,000 a year for those retiring before October 9, 1984, or $44,000 a year for those retiring on that date or later.

7. For a review of this literature, see L. A. Braskamp, D. C. Brandenburg, and J. C. Ory, *Evaluating Teaching Effectiveness: A Practical Guide* (Beverly Hills: Sage Publications, 1984); J. A. Centra, *Determining Faculty Effectiveness* (San Francisco: Jossey-Bass, 1979), 17–46; P. L. Peterson and H. J. Walberg, ed., *Research on Teaching: Concepts, Findings, and Implications* (Berkeley: McCutchan, 1980); and P. Seldin, *Successful Faculty Evaluation Programs A Practical Guide to Improve Faculty Performance and Promotion/Tenure* (Crugers, N.Y.: Coventry Press, 1980), 4–15 and 22–35.

8. This section draws heavily from this research, which was reported in D. P. Kinney and S. P. Smith, "Age and Teaching Performance" (unpublished paper, Industrial Relations Section, Princeton University, 1989).

9. See Centra (1979) and Seldin (1980) for an analytical review of the different measures available.

10. See Braskamp, Brandenburg, and Ory (1984, 35–47) and Centra (1979, 17–46) for a thorough review of these studies.

11. A student evaluation system has been in effect at this institution since academic year 1968–1969 and is applied to all undergraduate courses.

12. The explanatory variables are defined as follows: AGE = the chronological age of the instructor; REQUIRED = 1 if the course is required for graduation from a department within this institution; SHARED = 1 if the course is team taught; the "LEVEL" variables take the value 1 if the course is a low-, middle-, or upper-level course, with the entry-level course as the omitted base category; SMALLENR = 1 if the class has fewer than twenty students; and LARGEENR = 1 if the class has more than ninety students.

13. The variable "REQUIRED" was omitted because of lack of data, and a variable was included to account for the timing of the retirement decision. This variable, MANDRET, was set equal to 1 if the individual retired at the mandatory age.

14. In particular, this institution was able to collect data for tenured faculty in the arts and sciences only and to estimate equations—separately by broad discipline category—that specified evaluations as a function of the professor's age, the size of the class, and the level of the course (with these three different levels defined, but at different breakpoints than in the Kinney and Smith [1989] study). Some graduate student evaluations are included as well, but the percentages are small, as few graduate courses are offered in these areas. Information was not available on whether the course was required or team taught. The explanatory significance of these variables varied by discipline in the Kinney and Smith study. The data cover the two years in which the present evaluation instrument has been in use (a different instrument had been in use for the eight

years prior to this). Evaluations are also made on a five-point scale, with 0 labeled as "not applicable," 1 labeled as "low, poor," 5 labeled as "high, outstanding," and no labels applied to the intermediate values. The data sets here are larger, but the overall explanatory power of these equations is somewhat less than in the Kinney and Smith study. Moreover, these equations were estimated with ordinary least squares, whereas the Kinney and Smith analysis included the White (1980) correction for suspected heteroscedasticity. Despite these differences, we believe that this analysis offers a reasonable comparison with which to assess the applicability of the earlier study to other institutions.

15. It should be noted, however, that the relationship in the physical and biological sciences is very weak: Age is only marginally significant.

16. This section draws heavily from the research in another case study we sponsored, which was reported in A. B. Howe and S. P. Smith, "Age and Research Activity" (unpublished paper, Industrial Relations Section, Princeton University, 1991).

17. See, for example, P. D. Allison and J. A. Stewart, "Productivity Differences among Scientists: Evidence for Accumulative Advantage," *American Sociological Review* 39 (August 1974): 596–606; A. E. Bayer and J. E. Dutton, "Career Age and Research—Professional Activities of Academic Scientists: Tests of Alternative Nonlinear Models and Some Implications for Higher Education Faculty Policies," *Journal of Higher Education* 48 (May/June 1977): 259–82; J. A. Centra, *Determining Faculty Effectiveness* (San Francisco: Jossey-Bass, 1979); S. Cole, "Age and Scientific Performance," *American Journal of Sociology* 84 (January 1979): 958–77; D. Crane, "Scientists at Major and Minor Universities: A Study of Productivity and Recognition," *American Sociological Review* 30, no. 5 (1965): 699–713; J. W. Cresswell, ed., *Measuring Faculty Research Performance,* New Directions for Institutional Research no. 50 (San Francisco: Jossey-Bass, 1986); R. J. Havighurst, W. J. McDonald, L. Maeulen, and J. Mazel, "Male Social Scientists: Lives after Sixty," *Gerontologist* 19, no. 1 (1979): 55–60; Y. Neumann, "Standards of Research Publication: Differences between the Physical Sciences and the Social Sciences," *Research in Higher Education* 7 (1977): 355–77; B. R. Reskin, "Aging and Productivity: Careers and Results," in *Faculty Vitality and Institutional Productivity: Critical Perspectives for Higher Education,* edited by S. M. Clark and D. R. Lewis (New York: Teachers College Press, 1985), 86–97; D. K. Simonton, "Age and Outstanding Achievement: What Do We Know after a Century of Research?" *Psychological Bulletin* 104 (1988): 251–67; and H. Zuckerman, "The Sociology of Science," in *Handbook of Sociology,* edited by N. J. Smelser (Newbury Park, Cal.: Sage Publications, 1988).

18. It is important to recognize that these are not all-inclusive measures of research activities. Other tasks also constitute research activity but may be impossible to analyze across individuals: for example, refereeing journal articles or grant proposals and supervising graduate students engaged in research. Moreover, these activities are likely to increase with age and seniority and comprise a larger proportion of overall research activity.

19. It should be noted that there is no indication in either of these measures in the Carnegie data whether these activities are joint with other colleagues.

20. The division of departments into broad discipline categories in this study is somewhat different from that used elsewhere in this text or in the other case studies we have sponsored. The principal difference is that history is specified as a humanity rather than as a social science. No other division is possible because the Carnegie survey includes history in the single category "humanities," along with literature, philosophy, religion, theology, and rhetoric. Therefore, for consistency, history was excluded from the social sciences in the second data set, as well.

21. It might be suggested that simultaneity is a problem in these estimates because of the presence of the two preference variables, PRTEACH and PRRESEARCH, among the explanatory variables. However, this possibility was tested and found not to be a problem, which suggests that preferences toward teaching and for research are tastes developed over a lifetime and are not simultaneously determined with the output of research activity. For further discussion, see Howe and Smith (1991).

22. This section reflects preliminary findings of the project directed by Dean Robert McCaughey of Barnard College and funded by the Spencer Foundation, which have been generously shared with us. This study is an inquiry into the scholarly activities of faculty in the humanities and social sciences in thirteen Liberal Arts I colleges and one Research I university and examines publications and citations during a ten-year period. Because of the length of the period, it is not surprising that faculty under age 40 are observed to comprise a smaller proportion of the top quartile of number of publications than their proportion in the population.

23. The possibility of simultaneity in these regressions was also tested and again rejected, as in the relationship between publications and preferences. For further discussion, see Howe and Smith (1991).

24. In order to provide a uniform period of measurement for all faculty members, data were gathered only for those who were tenured at the beginning of the period and who did not exit from the institution (that is, resign, retire, or die) during the period.

25. For further details, see Howe and Smith (1991).

26. Similar evidence was found in data reported from another participating private Research I university on grant activity among retiring tenured faculty relative to their colleagues.

27. In particular, the peak occurred in the 46–50 cohort for the physical and biological sciences and in the 51–55 age cohort for the social sciences. Biedenweg and Shelley (1988, 62) observed a similar age profile in a recent analysis of the pattern of indirect cost recovery among faculty conducting sponsored research at Stanford University.

CHAPTER FIVE

Survey Results

IN THE course of the Project on Faculty Retirement we have conducted three small surveys, one of retired tenured faculty in the arts and sciences and two of active senior faculty (defined as tenured faculty between the ages of 55 and 70). We have also had access to several recent surveys done by others, some of which are comparable in whole or in part with ours. Some of these outside studies are not confined to the arts and sciences, and two deal only with law faculty. This chapter will attempt to summarize some of the salient results of all of these surveys.

SURVEYS OF RETIREES

The survey conducted as part of the project was of retired faculty in the arts and sciences at a private research university.[1] It covered surviving professors who retired between 1969 and 1988, a total of ninety-five people. Of these, seventy-four responded and seventy-one returned usable questionnaires. Interviews were conducted with thirty-seven of the respondents, usually by phone. The analysis was carried out separately for those who retired early (55 percent) and those who retired at the mandatory retirement age.

The same survey instrument was later used in a private doctorate-granting university; there were sixty-seven responses from the ninety-nine retired faculty members in the arts and sciences who were surveyed, or a 67 percent response rate. In Tables 5-1 through 5-5 and in the discussion below, the research university will be called "University I" and the other university will be called "University II."

The third survey of retirees is of retired law faculty.[2] This survey received 123 responses from law faculty who retired between 1984 and 1989, a response rate of about 45–50 percent. There are 175 law schools in the association whose retired faculty were surveyed.

The fourth study we review is a survey of faculty who retired under incentive early retirement programs at four institutions.[3] These include two public research universities, a public comprehensive college, and a small private college. The study received 314 responses from early re-

TABLE 5-1

Health Status of Retirees (percent)

	University I		University II		Law Schools
	Early	Mandatory	Early	Mandatory	
Excellent	23	9	49	13	45
Very good	36	31	26	35	
Good	33	53	23	31	} 46
Fair	—	—	—	—	7
Poor	5	6	3	17	
Very poor	2	0	0	4	} 2

Note: Percentages in this and the following tables may not total 100 or sum to the total shown because of rounding.

TABLE 5-2

Age at Which Respondent Would Choose to Retire Again (percent)

	University I		University II		Law Schools	Early Retirees (Four Schools)
	Early	Mandatory	Early	Mandatory		
Same age	69	66	66	27	62	77
Younger age	15	6	20	9	4	15
Older age	10	28	14	64	18	8
No response, other	6	0	—	—	2	—
Until health prevented	—	—	—	—	12	—

tirees, a response rate of 53 percent. The average age of respondents was only 62.

Table 5-1 summarizes the results of the three studies that report the health status of retirees. Although the categories are not exactly comparable, in all studies, fewer than a fourth of retirees report their health as poor, and in most cases fewer than 10 percent do so. This suggests that failing health is not a frequent reason for the retirement of faculty members.

Table 5-2 reports data from four studies on the age at which respondents would choose to retire if they had the decision to make over again. In all but one of the groups studied, a large majority of respondents would choose the same age. In the three groups of early retirees, more would select a still younger age than would select an older one.

TABLE 5-3
Retirement Income Compared to Final Income before Retirement
(percent)

	University I		
	Early	Mandatory	Law Schools
Below 75% of preretirement income	9	11	35
75–99% of preretirement income	30	26	30
100% of preretirement income	13	17	7
Above 100% of preretirement income	48	39	23
No reply	—	7	5

	University II	
	Early	Mandatory
Less than preretirement income	30	32
About the same as preretirement income	25	27
More than preretirement income	45	41

This weighting is reversed for the mandatory retirees and the law school retirees.

Table 5-3 shows data from three of the studies on retirement income as a percentage of final income before retirement. Except in the law schools, more retirees report a higher postretirement income than report a lower one. The survey questions refer to income from all sources; thus income from such sources as postretirement employment, royalties from books, and personal investments contribute to this result. The table also refers to nominal rather than real income. For those retired for some time, the results would be substantially less favorable if corrected for inflation.

The study of University I gives additional detail for those in the category "above 100 percent" in Table 5-3. Incomes of more than 175 percent of preretirement income were reported by 13 percent of the early retirees and 17 percent of the mandatory retirees; the highest figure reported was 350 percent.

81

TABLE 5-4
Postretirement Employment (percent)

	University I		University II		Law Schools	Early Retirees (Four Schools)
	Early	Mandatory	Early	Mandatory		
Full-time employment	12	3	—	—	14	9
Part-time employment	29	26	—	—	48	33
Occasional employment	3	10	—	—	—	15
Total	45	40	43	19	62	57

The corresponding question asked on the survey of early retirees in four institutions refers to standard of living rather than income. This differs from the income question because a previous standard of living can be maintained by spending down assets. Only 6 percent of the respondents in this survey reported a lower standard of living than before retirement; 72 percent reported the same standard of living, and 21 percent reported a higher one. The general conclusion that can be drawn from the data from all three surveys is that in the late 1980s, most faculty retirees appeared to have adequate retirement incomes.

Table 5-4 shows the percentage of responding retirees who had postretirement employment. Such employment was common, especially for early retirees, although part-time employment was more frequent than full-time employment. The fraction of retirees engaged in professional activity was much higher than the fraction employed for pay. In the survey of early retirees at four institutions, 81 percent reported being engaged in academic professional activities. More than 80 percent of both groups of retirees at University I reported being engaged in writing or educational pursuits. In University II, more than half of both groups reported such activity. This strong continued involvement in professional activity distinguishes retired faculty members from retired people in most other occupations.

Most retirees continued to have an association with the institution from which they had retired. In the survey of retirees from University I, more than half of all retirees continued to have office space, about a third had clerical support, and more than three-fourths had library privileges. The survey of retired law professors asked how often re-

TABLE 5-5
Satisfaction with Retirement as a Whole (percent)

	University I		University II		Law Schools	Early Retirees (Four Schools)
	Early	Mandatory	Early	Mandatory		
Very satisfied	72	44	71	43	60	66
Somewhat satisfied	23	53	29	48	16	28
Neither satis-fied nor dis-satisfied	—	—	—	—	6	5
Not satisfied	2	3	0	10	9	2
No response	3	—	—	—	9	—

tired faculty visited their law school and found that almost a third did so daily and more than half did so at least weekly.

A high proportion of retirees were also engaged in volunteer or community work. Half of the mandatory retirees and 41 percent of the early retirees at University I had been volunteers since they retired, and 80 percent of those still were volunteers. At University II, more than half of all respondents were volunteers. Half of retired law professors spent some time in volunteer or community work, and 59 percent of early retirees at four institutions were engaged in community or civic activities. Retirees also reported a wide variety of leisure and recreational activities, including gardening, hobbies, and travel.

Table 5-5 reports the results for the question "How satisfied are you with retirement as a whole?" The great majority of retirees reported that they were satisfied or very satisfied with retirement, but the level of satisfaction was higher among early retirees.

SURVEYS OF SENIOR FACULTY

Senior faculty are defined as tenured faculty aged 55–70. Surveys of senior faculty in the arts and sciences in two private research universities were done as part of the Project on Faculty Retirement.[4] The first of these universities is in the Carnegie classification Research I, and the second in the Carnegie classification Research II. Before these studies were begun, TIAA-CREF had done a large survey of its policyholders aged 55–70. We have used many of the same questions as did TIAA-

TABLE 5-6
Senior Faculty Having a Specific Retirement Age in Mind (percent)

	Research I University	Research II University	TIAA-CREF Survey	
			Public Universities	Private Universities
Have age in mind	50	59	71	73
No age in mind	32	24	13	15
Will work as long as possible	18	17	13	9
No response	—	—	3	3

CREF so that the results would be comparable. The published results of the TIAA-CREF study generally do not distinguish between faculty members and others, and more than half of the responses were not from faculty members.[5] However, TIAA-CREF has kindly made the data tapes from this study available to us, and from them we have been able to tabulate data for faculty members only, separately for public and private institutions. These data are not restricted to the arts and sciences. In addition, several individual universities have done their own surveys of senior faculty, and we have access to the results of some of these. They are not strictly comparable to ours and that of TIAA-CREF; the results will be mentioned in the text below when relevant, but not included in the tables. The same treatment will be given to a survey of senior law faculty.[6]

Some of the most important questions in the surveys of senior faculty deal with plans for retirement. Table 5-6 gives the results for a question dealing with whether or not the respondent has a specific retirement age in mind. Half or more of respondents in all four groups answer that they do have a specific retirement age in mind. For the two TIAA-CREF groups, more than 70 percent do so. The rest either have no age in mind or want to work as long as possible.

Table 5-7 shows a percentage distribution of the ages at which the people who answered that they had a specific age in mind expect to retire. The percentage expecting to retire before age 65 is substantially higher in the TIAA-CREF data than in the two research universities. In one of the two research universities, no one who had a specific age in mind expected to retire after age 70. In the other, only 13 percent of respondents expected to retire after age 70, and the corresponding TIAA-CREF percentages were even lower.

TABLE 5-7
Expected Age of Retirement (percent)

Age	Research I University	Research II University	TIAA-CREF Survey	
			Public Universities	Private Universities
60–64	10	13	26	23
65	23	26	23	19
66–69	32	26	25	26
70	36	23	19	26
Over 70	0	13	4	6
No answer	—	—	2	1

The same questions used in generating the data shown in Tables 5-6 and 5-7 were used by the University of California system in a survey of faculty aged 65–66 in the fall of 1989. This is the first group of faculty who will not be subject to mandatory retirement under the Age Discrimination in Employment Act as amended in 1986. The survey was sent to 130 faculty members, of whom 82 percent responded. About half had a specific retirement age in mind. The rest were asked to guess at a most likely retirement age. The results were analyzed by the University of California by combining the most likely and expected retirement ages. One-third of the respondents anticipated retiring between age 66 and age 69; 29 percent, at age 70; and 38 percent, at ages above 70. The mean anticipated age was 70.6 and the highest anticipated age was 85.[7] The higher proportion of respondents anticipating late retirement in the California survey as compared with the two research universities shown in Table 5-7 is explained by the fact that the California respondents are older than the average respondent in the other surveys. Those who planned to retire before age 60 had already done so and were therefore not in the sample that was surveyed.

A leading private research university has interviewed a random sample of forty-seven of its faculty aged 60 to 65, of whom 60 percent had a retirement age in mind. Of these, 35 percent intended to retire before age 70; about half, at age 70; and 14 percent, later than age 70.

In the survey of senior law faculty, 74 percent planned to retire at a specific age. Of these, 11 percent planned to retire between age 60 and age 64; 16 percent, at age 65; 14 percent, between age 66 and age 69; 44 percent, at age 70; and 15 percent, at age 71 or above. The highest expected age of retirement was 88. The percentage of senior law profes-

TABLE 5-8

Faculty Expectations about Their Standard of Living in Retirement (percent)

	Standard in First Year of Retirement Compared to Present		Standard in Sixth Year of Retirement Compared to Present	
	Public Universities	Private Universities	Public Universities	Private Universities
Better than now	6	8	6	6
About the same	67	58	47	41
Not as good	22	27	31	39
Much worse	1	2	5	5
Not certain	3	2	9	6

Source: TIAA-CREF data tapes.

sors expecting to retire at an age above 70 is somewhat greater than for the groups shown in Table 5-7.

The TIAA-CREF survey of policyholders asked respondents to rate several factors according to their importance in making the retirement decision. The most important single factor was the assurance of an adequate retirement income, which was rated as very important by 70 percent of the faculty respondents. Respondents were also asked about their expectations of their standard of living one year and six years after retirement, as compared with the present. The faculty responses to this question are shown in Table 5-8. More than half of those responding expected their standard of living one year after retirement to be about the same as their present one. This proportion is somewhat lower for private than for public institutions, and it falls off when the time horizon is lengthened. It is interesting to compare Table 5-8 with Table 5-3, based on replies from retired faculty. The proportion of those already retired whose income is greater than it was in the last year of teaching is far higher than the proportion of active senior faculty who expect to enjoy a higher standard of living in retirement. Two possible reasons for this large discrepancy occur to us. One is that active faculty expect a higher rate of inflation in the future than has prevailed in the recent past. The second and more probable is that faculty are simply not well informed about the incomes they can expect to receive from their retirement plans.

The second and third most important factors in the retirement decision according to the TIAA-CREF survey are the respondent's state of health and ability to perform his or her job up to his or her own expectations. Health was rated very important by 59 percent of faculty, and ability to perform up to one's own expectations was rated very important by 56 percent. These answers suggest that there may be some self-selection according to ability in early retirement decisions, with a tendency for less able faculty to retire earlier. Such a tendency is also suggested in some of the answers we have received from retirees to open-ended questions about reasons for retirement.

Two early retirees at the private university we studied put these thoughts in the following words:

> In the last two or three years . . . I was not as satisfied with the intellectual exchange with students. . . . I wasn't learning much.

> I originally thought I would retire at the mandatory age, but two or three years before I felt my energies decrease, so I decided to stop.

Those who had retired at the mandatory age often expressed quite opposite feelings. One stated:

> It was urgent for me to stay on. I was doing my best work in my late 60's. . . . I received more recognition than I had before. . . . but I had to leave because I reached the mandatory age.

The final source of survey data for senior faculty we have used is the survey done by the Carnegie Foundation for the Advancement of Teaching (see Chapter Four). This survey includes a question on the age at which the faculty member plans to retire. Because we have access to the full data tape, we can analyze the responses to this question by regressions across individuals.[8]

Table 5-9 shows the results of our best regression for senior faculty in the arts and sciences at four-year institutions. The dependent variable is expected age at retirement. All of the independent variables are zero-one dummies with the exception of the number of recent publications (publications within the last two years). The regression explains only 15 percent of the variance in expected age at retirement, but a number of the independent variables are statistically significant. The strongest are the dummy variables for two five-year age groups, 55–59 and 60–64 (the omitted category is age 65–69).[9] This is partly a mechanical effect, since those who planned to retire early in the oldest age groups have for the most part already done so, and thus are not in the sample. The dummy variable for research university adds more than half a year to the expected age at retirement and is marginally significant (6 percent

87

TABLE 5-9
Regression Analysis of Expected Age at Retirement

	Mean	Coefficient	t-Statistic
Expected age (dependent variable)	66.2	—	—
Constant	—	68.3	190.7
Research university	0.26	0.62	1.86
Defined-benefit pension plan	0.28	−0.97	−3.08
Major grant	0.24	−0.29	−0.82
Recent publications	2.53	0.10	2.31
Female	0.15	0.66	1.66
Age 55–59	0.53	−3.33	−8.74
Age 60–64	0.29	−1.72	−4.08

Adjusted R^2 = 0.149

N = 608

level). Surprisingly, female faculty members plan to retire more than half a year later than males, a finding that is marginally significant (10 percent level). Having a major grant does not produce a significant effect. Recent publications have a significant positive effect, adding a tenth of a year to the expected retirement age for each publication in the last two years. Finally, faculty members at institutions with defined-benefit pension plans expect to retire a year sooner than others, and this finding is clearly significant. There is thus a difference between our findings on the effects of the type of pension plan on actual age at retirement (see Chapter Two) and the finding reported here of its effect on expected retirement age as reported by senior faculty who have not yet retired.

NOTES

1. See Suzannah Bex Wilson, "The Implications of Eliminating Mandatory Retirement in Institutions of Higher Learning and Suggestions for Adapting to this Change: A Study of Retired Tenured Faculty" (unpublished paper, Industrial Relations Section, Princeton University, 1989).

2. See Judith A. McMorrow and Anthony Baldwin, "Survey of Retired Law Faculty," in *Report of the Special Committee on the Impact of the Elimination of*

Mandatory Retirement Requirements to the Association of American Law Schools (January, 1990).

3. See Samuel E. Kellams and Jay L. Chronister, *Life after Early Retirement: Faculty Activities and Perceptions,* Occasional Paper no. 14, Center for the Study of Higher Education, University of Virginia (1988).

4. See Elizabeth J. Carlson, "Mandatory Retirement and the Tenure Contract: A Study of Faculty Retirement Behavior" (unpublished paper, Industrial Relations Section, Princeton University, 1990).

5. See Kevin Gray, *Retirement Plans and Expectations of TIAA-CREF Policyholders* (New York: Teachers Insurance and Annuity Association/College Retirement Equities Fund, 1989).

Because this survey was sent out during the summer and instructed policyholders who had already retired not to complete the full form, it missed those who retired at the end of the spring term. It therefore severely understates the proportion of faculty who expect to retire at 65 and overstates the number who expect to retire at later ages. See Peggy Heim, "Age Patterns of Faculty Retirement in the 1990s," (paper presented to meeting of the American Association for Higher Education, Spring 1990).

6. See David S. Day, Thomas Langham, and Susan Pearson, "Survey of Senior Law Faculty," in *Report of the Special Committee on the Impact of the Elimination of Mandatory Retirement Requirements to the Association of American Law Schools* (1990).

7. See the Appendix to the Interim Report of the Task Force on Mandatory Retirement, University of California, Office of the President (Berkeley: April 1990).

8. An analysis of the expected age of retirement from this survey appears in Carnegie Foundation for the Advancement of Teaching, "Early Faculty Retirees: Who, Why, and with What Impact?" *Change,* July/August 1990. This analysis uses descriptive statistics covering faculty members of all ages at all institutions and in all fields. The focus is on early retirement, defined as retirement before age 63. Our regressions cover faculty members aged 55 and over at four-year institutions in the arts and sciences only.

9. Most faculty members aged 65 to 69 in 1989 at capped institutions will be required to retire at age 70 because the end of mandatory retirement for tenured faculty under federal law does not occur until 1994. This in itself should make the expected age of retirement lower for the omitted group than for the other two groups, which is the reverse of what we find.

CHAPTER SIX

Conclusions

IN THE preceding chapters, we have described the results of an investigation into the probable effects on higher education in the arts and sciences of the 1986 amendments to the Age Discrimination in Employment Act, which will abolish mandatory retirement for tenured faculty at colleges and universities effective January 1, 1994. This investigation has relied heavily on the natural experiment afforded by the fact that mandatory retirement of tenured faculty is already unlawful in several states under state law. We will now set forth our conclusions and policy recommendations. In doing so, we may at times go beyond the strict confines of our data, and draw more broadly on our experience in higher education. We shall be speaking only for ourselves, not for our sponsoring organizations, our advisory committee, or the foundations that have provided our funding.

The passage of the 1986 amendments was viewed by the higher education community with considerable alarm. Shortly before their passage, the prestigious Commission on College Retirement wrote, "Government intervention to 'uncap' the retirement age would imperil academic freedom since regular performance evaluations of all tenured faculty would become inevitable."[1] Similar statements of concern were made by a number of leading university administrators after the passage of the amendments.

Our principal conclusion is that these statements of alarm and concern have surprisingly little basis in fact. If professors in the future behave as do those in institutions already uncapped under state law, the impact of uncapping will be much smaller than has been anticipated. It is possible that the impact will increase over time, but it should be noted that some of our data come from institutions that have been uncapped for more than a decade. A return to double-digit inflation could magnify the effect of uncapping by raising new fears about the decline of real income in retirement, as could a sustained decline in the stock market, by reducing the value of accumulations in the College Retirement Equities Fund.

In any event, we do not mean to say that the end of mandatory retirement will cause no problems. A single incompetent professor is a severe problem for his or her students, colleagues, and institution. But we find no evidence to suggest that any considerable number of those who choose to stay on beyond age 70 will in fact be incompetent. More important, we believe that the large majority of professors whose work is unsatisfactory will be below age 70, simply because the number choosing to stay beyond 70 will be so small. This conclusion is based largely on the evidence presented in Chapter Two that there is no significant difference in mean retirement age between capped and uncapped public universities or capped and uncapped liberal arts colleges.

This conclusion should hold for most of the institutions in the groups we have studied: doctorate-granting universities and selective liberal arts colleges. It should hold still more strongly for those we have not studied—comprehensive institutions and less selective colleges, where evidence from other studies indicates that retirement ages will be even lower. Nevertheless, there are a few institutions that will have substantial problems: those whose faculty now generally choose to retire at the mandatory age of 70. In our sample, all of these are private research universities. Within this group, they are some of the most prestigious and selective, and are among the few that have not had generous incentive early retirement plans. We shall make some suggestions for these institutions later in this chapter.

One of the sources of concern about uncapping is that it will reduce institutional vitality by producing an aging tenured faculty with less room for new blood. Somewhat to our surprise, we find no support for this concern. In Chapter Three, we have made projections of the age distributions of tenured faculty in the arts and sciences to the year 2004. Making the extremely conservative assumption that there is no growth in the size of the tenured faculty and that the retention rate in the oldest cohorts is 50 percent higher than we now observe in uncapped institutions, we still project a higher proportion of tenured faculty under age 40 in every class of institution. The effects of delayed retirement for part of the oldest cohorts is simply outweighed by other aspects of faculty demography.

Underlying the concern about uncapping is the belief that faculty productivity declines with age after midcareer. In Chapter Four, we have reviewed and extended the evidence on the relationship between age and research productivity, and have for the first time furnished some statistical evidence on the relationship between age and teaching effectiveness. The evidence that research productivity in general decreases after midcareer is very consistent. But research output does not

91

disappear completely late in an academic career. Professors in their sixties still publish, although less than they did before. All this implies that an increase in the number of faculty members in their 70s could lead to some overall reduction in research productivity. It is not clear, however, that this poses serious problems for the universities that employ older faculty members. It is, of course, an important part of the mission of a university to add to knowledge. But individual universities are also greatly concerned with enhancing their prestige as institutions. From this perspective, a faculty member's lifetime research output may be more important than his or her current output. Lifetime output is the basis of reputation, which lags behind achievement, and it is reputation that helps in recruiting graduate students and junior colleagues. A faculty member who is no longer active in research may also still be productively involved in teaching and administration.

The real specter that haunts college and university administrators is that of the incompetent teacher—the aging professor who totters up to the podium and delivers a soporific lecture from notes that have not been revised in twenty years. Our evidence on the relationship between age and teaching effectiveness is much more mixed than that on research productivity. First, age does not seem to be a very large factor in student evaluations of teaching effectiveness. Moreover, the patterns are not the same for different disciplines. Although teaching effectiveness seems to decline after midcareer for scientists, the evidence is mixed for humanists, while for social scientists teaching effectiveness seems to rise in their 60s. This evidence tends to support our view that the number of ineffective elderly faculty members will not be large.

We turn now to some of the specific proposals that have been made for coping with problems that may be created by uncapping. One of these is the suggestion for formal posttenure review. We know of one large university system—the University of California—that uses periodic posttenure review, using much the same standards and procedures that are used for the initial granting of tenure. On one campus where a backlog of reviews had accumulated, sixty faculty members were reviewed in one year, and five of these, all over age 55, were determined to be "grossly incompetent." Of these, three retired and the possibility of dismissal was being considered for the others.

The California experience makes clear that formal posttenure review can be used to identify incompetent faculty members. However, it also makes clear that the process, if conducted rigorously, is enormously costly in terms of faculty and administrative time. Many institutions will decide that the benefits do not outweigh these costs. In smaller institutions, it seems likely that chairs and deans know who the incompetent faculty members are without going through a formal review process. Although incompetence has always been a ground for revoking tenure, very few dismissals have been attempted. In part this is because the process of dismissal is inherently distasteful, and in part it is because affording the faculty member due process, involving careful documentation of all charges, can be lengthy and costly. The end of mandatory retirement may increase the number of such cases, even absent formal posttenure review. At present, the realization that a 66-year-old professor is incompetent may not precipitate any action by the administration, since he or she will retire anyway in four more years. The prospect that he or she might choose to stay six or eight more years could lead administrators to face the problem earlier.

A step beyond the concept of posttenure review is the proposal to replace lifetime tenure with a series of fixed-term contracts. If the term of these contracts is short, the protection afforded to faculty members by tenure would be seriously eroded, and even long contracts would not fully protect the freedoms protected by tenure. Oscar M. Ruebhausen proposes a long-term contract, from twenty to thirty-five years at the option of the faculty member.[2] But if a faculty member appointed to a tenured position at age 35 is allowed to select a contract of thirty-five years, will the same option be offered to a faculty member appointed to a tenured position at age 50? If not, does not the arrangement itself on its face violate the Age Discrimination in Employment Act?

We are not lawyers, and others more qualified than we are exploring these issues. Our point is a different one. The number of faculty members likely to teach beyond age 70 after uncapping and the number of years beyond age 70 that they are likely to continue teaching do not seem to us to be large enough to warrant in themselves making substantial changes in tenure arrangements developed over a long period of years for an important purpose, protecting academic freedom, and widely accepted in the higher education community. It is not our intention to review here the whole debate over whether or not there should be academic tenure, although we personally favor it. But if tenure arrangements should be changed, it should not be because of the 1986 amendments to ADEA, but for some more fundamental reason.

A third policy suggestion for coping with the 1986 amendments is to replace defined-contribution pension plans with defined-benefit plans, on the ground that absent mandatory retirement, defined-contribution plans offer too large a financial incentive to delay retirement. We noted in Chapter Two that the advocates of this position seem to underestimate the extent to which the defined-benefit plans in present use in higher education offer similar incentives. It is nevertheless true that at moderate rates of salary increase (6 percent or less), defined-contribution plans offer a larger reward for teaching an additional year. We therefore compared the mean age of retirement at public universities with defined-benefit plans with that at public universities with defined-contribution plans and found almost no difference between the two groups. This suggests that the existence of incentives does not always mean that large numbers of people will respond to them. It is true that our results are based on a small sample of institutions. However, we know of no other results that hold the type of institution constant, and unless this is done, no valid conclusion can be drawn from the comparison. We should also note that we did find that a defined-contribution pension plan increases the age at which senior faculty say they plan to retire (see Chapter Five).

Defined-contribution plans offer very important advantages both to the faculty member and to the institution. To the faculty member, the advantages include immediate vesting of all contributions and complete portability. Neither of these benefits is available in existing defined-benefit plans, although better ones could no doubt be devised. For the institution, the defined-contribution plan offers the great advantage that the faculty member bears all the investment risk. There can be no such thing as an underfunded defined-contribution plan, while there are large numbers of severely underfunded defined-benefit plans in American industry.

Given our estimates of the probable effects of the 1986 ADEA amendments, we cannot recommend that institutions that currently have defined-contribution plans should terminate them and replace them with defined-benefit plans. We do see some evidence from our surveys of retirees that defined-contribution plans in some institutions have provided higher retirement benefits than was originally intended. This, of course, can be corrected by reducing the rate of contribution without shifting to a defined-benefit plan. However, to make the plans less generous now could increase the number of faculty members who choose to teach beyond 70.

Let us now return to the case of the few institutions that will confront the possibility that many faculty members will choose to teach beyond age 70. The extreme case in our sample is a private research university where 73 percent of retiring faculty members in the arts and sciences retire at the mandatory age. What can such an institution do if it prefers not to have many of these teach three or four more years? We have three suggestions.

The first is that such institutions review the benefits offered to retired faculty and see whether they can be improved at reasonable cost. For example, can the institution afford to guarantee that these professors can keep offices in close proximity to their departments? We can think of nothing more likely to delay retirement for a scholar than the prospect of being relocated to some remote academic Siberia. Do all retired faculty have access to secretarial help and to computing facilities? If not, would better provisions be advisable?

Our second suggestion is that these institutions consider an incentive early retirement plan or a partial retirement plan if they do not already have one, and consider improving these plans if they do. The evidence presented in Chapter Two suggests, though not decisively, that on average such plans reduce mean age at retirement by about a year. We are aware that such plans can be very expensive, and for many colleges and universities they are not worth what they cost. The universities under discussion here may be the exceptions to that rule. We are also aware that some such plans have been terminated because in the opinion of counsel they were in violation of the Age Discrimination in Employment Act. However, many of the legal problems of these plans may have been resolved by the passage of the Older Workers Benefit Protection Act in October 1990.

Third, it is our impression, which we cannot document, that the institutions with the highest rates of retirement at the mandatory age are those in which the most senior faculty have the lightest teaching duties, both because a large part of their duties consist of research and because the teaching they do consists largely of graduate seminars or small upper-division courses in their fields of specialization. These institutions may want to make sure that teaching duties are equitably shared among faculty members of all ages, with the most senior faculty teaching their fair share of introductory courses. Among its other virtues, such a distribution of duties might improve teaching, since the youngest faculty members, who are the most recently trained, are often the most qualified to teach the most advanced courses, while the most senior faculty have the broad perspectives of their fields that enrich introductory courses.

Finally, we turn to the question of whether the higher education associations should ask Congress to amend the Age Discrimination Act once again so as to delay the end of mandatory retirement for tenured faculty beyond 1994. It is clear that the organizations representing higher education were opposed to ending mandatory retirement for what were on the whole good reasons. Their preferences have undoubtedly not changed. But it no longer seems clear that the end of mandatory retirement for tenured faculty will bring severe problems to much of higher education. On the contrary, most of higher education will not be seriously affected. The few universities that will feel a serious impact are among those with the largest endowments. In our opinion, it is quite unlikely that an appeal to Congress on behalf of these institutions would be successful, and therefore we believe that it should not be made.

NOTES

1. Commission on College Retirement, *Retirement Ages for College and University Personnel* (January 1986), 42.
2. See Ruebhausen 1989.

Advisory Committee to the Project on Faculty Retirement

Ernst Benjamin
General Secretary
American Association of University
   Professors

Derek Bok
President
Harvard University

Ralph S. Brown
Professor Emeritus
Yale Law School

Robert A. Bryan
Provost and Vice President for
   Academic Affairs
University of Florida

Robert L. Clodius
President
National Association of State
   Universities and Land-Grant
   Colleges

Matthew W. Finkin
College of Law
University of Illinois

Mary W. Gray
Chair, Department of Mathematics
American University

Katharine H. Hanson
Executive Director
Consortium on Financing Higher
   Education

Nils Hasselmo
Senior Vice President and Provost
University of Arizona

John Lombardi
Provost
Johns Hopkins University

Linda Lorimer
President
Randolph-Macon Woman's College

Francis C. Oakley
President
Williams College

Robert M. O'Neill
President
University of Virginia

Sherwin Rosen
Department of Economics
University of Chicago

Robert M. Rosenzweig
President
Association of American
   Universities

James N. Rosse
Vice President/Provost
Stanford University

Harold T. Shapiro
President
Princeton University

97

Charles E. Young
Chancellor
University of California, Los Angeles

Titles and affiliations are those that were effective at the time of appointment to the Advisory Committee.

Institutions Included in the Final Sample

PRIVATE UNIVERSITIES: CAPPED

American University
Cornell University
Duke University
Harvard University
Princeton University
Stanford University
Tufts University
University of Chicago
University of Southern California
Vanderbilt University
Yale University

PUBLIC UNIVERSITIES: CAPPED

University of California, Berkeley
University of Georgia
University of Michigan, Ann Arbor

PUBLIC UNIVERSITIES: UNCAPPED

University of Connecticut
University of Florida
University of Maine
University of Virginia
University of Wisconsin, Madison

LIBERAL ARTS COLLEGES: CAPPED

Amherst College
Barnard College
Bennington College
Carleton College
Colgate University
Davidson College
Smith College

LIBERAL ARTS COLLEGES:
UNCAPPED

Bates College
Beloit College
Bowdoin College
Colby College
Lawrence University
Middlebury College
Ripon College

Capped institutions are those that had a mandatory retirement age in the last year of the data set; uncapped institutions are those that did not. All private universities are capped.

Broad Discipline Categories
Used in This Study

HUMANITIES

Art
Art History
Archaeology
Classics
Comparative Literature
Creative Writing
English
Foreign Languages and Literature
Linguistics
Music
Philosophy
Religion

SOCIAL SCIENCES

Anthropology
Demography
Economics
Geography
History

Political Science
Psychology
Sociology

PHYSICAL AND BIOLOGICAL
SCIENCES

Astronomy
Astrophysical Sciences
Biology
Biochemical Sciences
Botany
Chemistry
Computer Science
Geological and Geophysical Sciences
Mathematics
Microbiology
Neuroscience
Physics
Planetary Science
Statistics
Zoology

Selected References

Allison, Paul D. 1984. *Event History Analysis Regression for Longitudinal Event Data*. Beverly Hills: Sage Publications.

Allison, Paul D., and John A. Stewart. 1974. "Productivity Differences among Scientists: Evidence for Accumulative Advantage." *American Sociological Review* 39 (August): 596–606.

American Association of University Professors. Committee A on Academic Freedom and Tenure. 1989. "Faculty Tenure and the End of Mandatory Retirement." *Academe*, September/October, 48.

Bayer, Alan E., and Jeffrey E. Dutton. 1977. "Career Age and Research—Professional Activities of Academic Scientists: Tests of Alternative Nonlinear Models and Some Implications for Higher Education Faculty Policies." *Journal of Higher Education* 48, no. 3 (May/June): 259–82.

Berkowitz, Monroe. 1985. "Over the Hill and under the Weather: Age v. Health." In *The Economics of Aging*, edited by Myron H. Ross, 113–38. Kalamazoo, Mich.: W. E. Upjohn Institute for Employment Research.

Biedenweg, Rick, and Tom Keenan. 1989. *The Faculty COHORT Model User Manual*.

Biedenweg, Rick, and Dana Shelley. 1988. *1986–1987 Decanal Indirect Cost Study*. Stanford University.

Blackburn, Robert T. 1985. "Faculty Career Development: Theory and Practice." In *Faculty Vitality and Institutional Productivity: Critical Perspectives for Higher Education*, edited by Shirley M. Clark and Darrell R. Lewis, 55–85. New York: Teachers College Press.

Bodie, Zvi. 1990. "Pensions as Retirement Income Insurance." *Journal of Economic Literature* 28, no. 1: 28–49.

Bowen, Howard R., and Jack H. Schuster. 1986. *American Professors: A National Resource Imperiled*. New York: Oxford University Press.

Bowen, William G., and Julie Ann Sosa. 1989. *Prospects for Faculty in the Arts and Sciences: A Study of Factors Affecting Demand and Supply, 1987 to 2012*. Princeton: Princeton University Press.

Braskamp, Larry A., Dale C. Brandenburg, and John C. Ory. 1984. *Evaluating Teaching Effectiveness: A Practical Guide*. Beverly Hills: Sage Publications.

Brown, Ralph S., B. Robert Kreiser, Joel T. Rosenthal, and Peter O. Steiner (Subcommittee of Committee A on Academic Freedom and Tenure of the American Association of University Professors) 1987. "Working Paper on the Status of Tenure without Mandatory Retirement." *Academe*, July/August, 45–48.

Carlson, Elizabeth J. 1990. "Mandatory Retirement and the Tenure Contract: A

Study of Faculty Retirement Behavior." Unpublished paper, Industrial Relations Section, Princeton University.

Carnegie Council on Policy Studies in Higher Education. 1980. *Three Thousand Futures*. San Francisco. Cited in Bowen and Schuster 1986.

Carnegie Foundation for the Advancement of Teaching. 1987. *A Classification of Institutions of Higher Education*. A Carnegie Foundation Technical Report. Princeton.

———. 1989. *The Condition of the Professoriate: Attitudes and Trends*. A Carnegie Foundation Technical Report. Princeton.

———. 1990. "Early Faculty Retirees: Who, Why and with What Impact?" *Change* 22, no. 4 (July/August): 31–34.

Centra, John A. 1979. *Determining Faculty Effectiveness*. San Francisco: Jossey-Bass.

Chronister, Jay L., and Thomas R. Kepple, Jr. 1987. *Incentive Early Retirement Programs for Faculty*. ASHE-ERIC Education Report no. 1. Washington, D.C.: Association for the Study of Higher Education (ASHE).

Clark, Shirley M., Carol M. Boyer, and Mary Corcoran. 1985. "Faculty and Institutional Vitality in Higher Education." In *Faculty Vitality and Institutional Productivity: Critical Perspectives for Higher Education*, edited by Shirley M. Clark and Darrell R. Lewis, 3–24. New York: Teachers College Press.

Cole, Stephen. 1979. "Age and Scientific Performance." *American Journal of Sociology* 84, no. 4 (January): 958–77.

Commission on College Retirement. 1986. *Retirement Ages for College and University Personnel*. Mimeo, January.

———. 1990. *Pension and Retirement Policies in Colleges and Universities*. San Francisco: Jossey-Bass.

Crane, Diane. 1965. "Scientists at Major and Minor Universities: A Study of Productivity and Recognition." *American Sociological Review* 30, no. 5: 699–713.

Cresswell, John W., ed. 1986. *Measuring Faculty Research Performance*. New Directions for Institutional Research no. 50. San Francisco: Jossey-Bass.

Daniels, Craig E., and Janet D. Daniels. 1990. "Voluntary Retirement Incentive Options in Higher Education." *Benefits Quarterly* 6, no. 2 (2d quarter): 68–78.

Day, David S., Thomas Langham, and Susan Pearson. 1990. "Survey of Senior Law Faculty." In *Report of the Special Committee on the Impact of the Elimination of Mandatory Retirement Requirements to the Association of American Law Schools*. January.

DiGiovanni, Nicholas, Jr. 1989. *Age Discrimination: An Administrator's Guide*. Washington, D.C.: College and University Personnel Association.

Feldt, James A. 1986. "Markov Models and Reductions in Work Force." In *Applying Decision Support Systems in Higher Education*, edited by John Rohrbaugh and Anne Taylor McCartt, 29–42. New Directions for Institutional Research no. 49. San Francisco: Jossey-Bass.

Finkin, Matthew W. 1989. "Tenure after the ADEA Amendments: A Different View." In *The End of Mandatory Retirement: Effects on Higher Education*, edited by Karen C. Holden and W. Lee Hansen, 97–111. New Directions for Higher Education no. 65. San Francisco: Jossey-Bass.

Garvin, David A. 1980. *The Economics of University Behavior*. New York: Academic Press.

Gray, Kevin. 1989. *Retirement Plans and Expectations of TIAA-CREF Policyholders*. New York: Teachers Insurance and Annuity Association/College Retirement Equities Fund.

Hansen, W. Lee, and Karen C. Holden. 1981. *Mandatory Retirement in Higher Education*. Unpublished report for the U.S. Department of Labor. Department of Economics, University of Wisconsin.

Havighurst, Robert J. 1985. "Aging and Productivity: The Case of Older Faculty." In *Faculty Vitality and Institutional Productivity: Critical Perspectives for Higher Education*, edited by Shirley M. Clark and Darrell R. Lewis, 98–111. New York: Teachers College Press.

Havighurst, Robert J., William J. McDonald, Leo Maeulen, and Joseph Mazel. 1979. "Male Social Scientists: Lives after Sixty." *Gerontologist* 19, no. 1: 55–60.

Heil, Mark T. 1990. "An Analysis of the Implications of Eliminating Mandatory Retirement in Institutions of Higher Education: A Study of Retired Tenured Faculty." Unpublished paper, Industrial Relations Section, Princeton University.

Heim, Peggy. 1990. "Age Patterns of Faculty Retirement in the 1990's." Paper presented at meeting of the American Association for Higher Education. Spring.

Hill, M. Anne. 1988. "An Examination of Retirement Patterns and the Age Distribution of Faculty in Public Higher Education in New Jersey." Bureau of Economic Research, Rutgers University.

Howe, Alan B., and Sharon P. Smith. 1991. "Age and Research Activity." Unpublished paper, Industrial Relations Section, Princeton University.

Kellams, Samuel E., and Jay L. Chronister. 1988. *Life after Early Retirement: Faculty Activities and Perceptions*. Occasional Paper no. 14, Center for the Study of Higher Education, University of Virginia.

Kinney, Daniel P., and Sharon P. Smith. 1989. "Age and Teaching Performance." Unpublished paper, Industrial Relations Section, Princeton University.

Lozier, G. Gregory, and Michael J. Dooris. 1991. *Faculty Retirement Projections beyond 1994: Effects of Policy on Individual Choice*. Boulder, Colo.: Western Interstate Commission for Higher Education.

McMorrow, Judith A., and Anthony Baldwin. 1990. "Survey of Retired Law Faculty." In *Report of the Special Committee on the Impact of the Elimination of Mandatory Retirement Requirements to the Association of American Law Schools*. January.

105

Neumann, Yoram. 1977. "Standards of Research Publication: Differences between the Physical Sciences and the Social Sciences." *Research in Higher Education* 7: 355–67.

Nevison, Christopher H. 1980. "Effects of Tenure and Retirement Policies on the College Faculty: A Case Study Using Computer Simulation." *Journal of Higher Education* 51, no. 2: 150–66.

Peterson, P. L., and H. J. Walberg, eds. 1980. *Research on Teaching: Concepts, Findings, and Implications*. Berkeley: McCutchan.

Planning Council, University of Minnesota. 1980. "A Proposal for a Study on 'The Future Vitality of the Faculties of the University.'" Memorandum to President C. Peter Magrath, University of Minnesota. February 11. Cited in Clark, Boyer, and Corcoran 1985.

Reskin, Barbara R. 1977. "Scientific Productivity and the Reward Structure of Science." *American Sociological Review* 42 (June): 491–504.

————. "Aging and Productivity: Careers and Results." 1985. In *Faculty Vitality and Institutional Productivity: Critical Perspectives for Higher Education*, edited by Shirley M. Clark and Darrell R. Lewis, 86–97. New York: Teachers College Press.

Rosovsky, Henry. 1990. *The University: an Owner's Manual*. New York: W. W. Norton & Company.

Ruebhausen, Oscar M. 1989. "Implications of the 1986 ADEA Amendments for Tenure and Retirement." In *The End of Mandatory Retirement: Effects on Higher Education*, edited by Karen C. Holden and W. Lee Hansen, 85–95. New Directions for Higher Education no. 65. San Francisco: Jossey-Bass.

Seldin, Peter. 1980. *Successful Faculty Evaluation Programs: A Practical Guide to Improve Faculty Performance and Promotion/Tenure Decisions*. Congers, N.Y.: Coventry Press.

Simonton, Dean Keith. 1988. "Age and Outstanding Achievement: What Do We Know after a Century of Research?" *Psychological Bulletin* 104, no. 2: 251–67.

Stephan, Paula E., and Sharon G. Levin. 1987. *Demographic and Economic Determinants of Scientific Productivity*. National Science Foundation Report. November.

Task Force on Mandatory Retirement, University of California, Office of the President, Berkeley. 1990. Appendix to the Interim Report. April.

U. S. Department of Health and Human Services. Public Health Service. Alcohol, Drug Abuse, and Mental Health Administration. Division of Program Analysis. Office of Extramural Programs. 1988. *Age Trends of ADAMHA Principal Investigators*. ADAMHA Program, Analysis Report, Report no. 88–10.

White, Halbert. 1980. "Nonlinear Regression on Cross-Section Data." *Econometrica* 48 (April): 721–46.

Wilson, Suzannah Bex. 1989. "The Implications of Eliminating Mandatory Retirement in Institutions of Higher Learning and Suggestions for Adapting to this Change: A Study of Retired Tenured Faculty." Unpublished paper, Industrial Relations Section, Princeton University.

Zuckerman, Harriet. 1988. "The Sociology of Science." In *Handbook of Sociology*, edited by N. J. Smelser, 511–74. Newbury Park, Cal.: Sage Publications.

DATE DUE
